ALL FLAGS FLYING

Glorious Lady Freedom by Moneca Calvert, Carmichael, California. 1985–1986. 72″ x 71½″. Cotton, cotton blends, polyester, and linens. This quilt is the Grand Prize winner in The Great American Quilt Contest held in celebration of the Statue of Liberty Centennial. A personal visit to the Statue of Liberty in 1982 had a profound effect on the artist. "If I had not seen that statue myself I could not have done this quilt. Being from the West, I didn't know what to expect. I was overwhelmed. I learned so much about myself and my country. I am not a flag-waver, but I discovered I am a serious American. When I was thinking about the design I would use, I recalled the words of the song, 'America the Beautiful.' It is all there in my piece. There is something for every American." Moneca Calvert has been seriously involved in the quilt world since 1980. She is a member of several local and national quilt guilds and societies and has been sharing her special skills with others by teaching for the past year. She worked about twelve hours a day for over six months to complete this quilt. She is not shy about her lack of a formal artistic education. "I guess I have the right to call myself an artist now. This is very exciting for your plain old average American." (Museum of American Folk Art: The Scotchgard® Collection of Contemporary Quilts)

ALL FLAGS FLYING

AMERICAN PATRIOTIC QUILTS AS EXPRESSIONS OF LIBERTY

Robert Bishop and Carter Houck

PHOTOGRAPHY OF ALL CONTEST QUILTS BY SCHECTER LEE

E. P. DUTTON   NEW YORK
In association with the
MUSEUM OF AMERICAN FOLK ART   NEW YORK

NOTE ABOUT DETAIL ILLUSTRATIONS

Page i: detail from figure 41, page 39

Page v: detail from figure 55, page 48

Page vii: detail from figure 4, page 14

Page viii: detail from figure 16, page 23

Page 5: detail from figure 8, page 17

Page 6: detail from figure 6, page 15

Page 52: detail from figure 12, page 20

Book design by Marilyn Rey

First published, 1986, in the United States by E. P. Dutton. / All rights reserved under International and Pan-American Copyright Conventions. / No part of this book may be reproduced or transmitted in any form or by any means, electronic or mechanical, including photocopy, recording, or any storage and retrieval system now known or to be invented, without permission in writing from the publishers, except by a reviewer who wishes to quote brief passages in connection with a review written for inclusion in a magazine, newspaper, or broadcast. / Published simultaneously in Canada by Fitzhenry & Whiteside Limited, Toronto. / W / Published in the United States by E. P. Dutton, a division of New American Library, 2 Park Avenue, New York, N.Y. 10016. / Printed and bound by Dai Nippon Printing Co., Ltd., Tokyo, Japan. / Library of Congress Catalog Card Number: 85-73525. / ISBN: 0-525-24414-X (cloth); ISBN: 0-525-48214-8 (DP).
10 9 8 7 6 5 4 3 2

CONTENTS

Spacious Skies by Charlotte Warr-Andersen, Kearns, Utah. 1985–1986. 72″ x 71½″. Cotton fabrics with some polyester blends used because the maker could not obtain all the hues she desired in 100% cotton materials. This quilt was the Second Prize winner in The Great American Quilt Contest held in celebration of the Statue of Liberty Centennial. The artist purposely chose pastel shades for her appliqué work, which includes a central figure of Liberty surrounded by vignettes of Mt. Rushmore, South Dakota; The Golden Gate Bridge, San Francisco, California; the Raising of the Flag at Iwo Jima; and the Moon Walk. The selection of these particular scenes was an attempt by the maker to "show how America has left its mark of freedom and liberty upon our own land, the world, and beyond." Liberty's tiara is repeated as a design motif in the top and bottom borders. Charlotte Warr-Andersen teaches needle arts at the Pioneer Craft House in Salt Lake City, Utah. She believes "quilts are a valid artistic expression. I feel more like an artist than I do a quiltmaker. I prefer to be called a quilt artist." This quilt took nearly 1,000 hours to complete. (Museum of American Folk Art: The Scotchgard® Collection of Contemporary Quilts)

FOREWORD

If ever there were a reason for quilt enthusiasts to celebrate the remarkable skills, creativity, and craftsmanship of the American needlewoman, the time is now. The Great American Quilt Festival, a Museum of American Folk Art event presented by Scotchgard® brand products in celebration of the Statue of Liberty Centennial, brought together in New York City in April 1986 an unprecedented number of antique-quilt exhibitions and related displays. It was a special pleasure for me to have served as Honorary Chairperson for this unique project.

The very best contemporary quilting efforts were also highly visible at The Great American Quilt Festival. Fifty-two prize-winning quilts—one from each state, and two from United States territories—were selected by twenty-eight regional and national judges from The Great American Quilt Contest. These are illustrated in the second section of this book, *All Flags Flying*, written by Robert Bishop and Carter Houck. To place these dazzling examples of modern needlework in historical context, Carter Houck selected a rich display of patriotic quilts from earlier times. Her handsome selection opens this volume.

As Honorary Chairperson of The Great American Quilt Festival, I was pleased to have had an opportunity of calling attention to the best quilts from the past, of creating awareness for the efforts of the finest quiltmakers of today, and of playing a role in preserving this rich legacy for the future. With *All Flags Flying* we salute the remarkable contributions to our artistic heritage by American needlewomen from all generations.

BARBARA BUSH

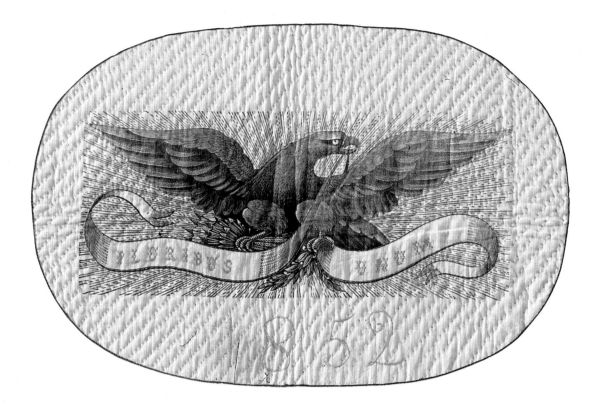

Quilts are a uniquely American art form which chronicle significant events and family traditions in colorful swatches of fabric and needlework. That's why 3M, through its Scotchgard® Brand Products Group, is proud to sponsor The Great American Quilt Contest and Festival.

With its theme of "Liberty, Freedom and the American Heritage in Honor of the Statue of Liberty Centennial," the Contest and Festival recognize the proud principles on which our nation was founded. The events also salute contemporary quiltmakers who carry on a proud American heritage.

We salute the thousands of quilters from across the land who stitched quilts to honor The Lady that stands at the doorway to our nation as a symbol of freedom and opportunity. One of the most important legacies we can pass on to future generations is the gift of their heritage, remembered and preserved. These quilts express the American heritage of the 1980s in a most colorful and dramatic fashion.

ALLEN F. JACOBSON
Chairman and Chief Executive Officer
U. S. Operations
3M Company

INTRODUCTION

Barbara Bush, Honorary Chairperson of The Great American Quilt Festival, wrote in her foreword to this book, "With *All Flags Flying* we salute the remarkable contributions to our artistic heritage by American needlewomen from all generations."

What a fitting tribute to the many women whose very lives are stitched into the patriotic quilts selected by Carter Houck for the first section of this book, and to the contemporary needleworkers whose prize-winning quilts from The Great American Quilt Contest are illustrated in the second section called "Expressions of Liberty."

The idea for a national contest and quilt festival was developed when Bruce Marsh, an account executive with a public relations firm visited the Museum of American Folk Art in New York City. He wished to discuss ways in which the 3M corporation of St. Paul, Minnesota, might assist the Museum by sponsoring an exhibition or with some other project and at the same time attract attention for one of their products, Scotchgard® brand fabric protector. Bruce had become aware of our institution through an article in an in-flight magazine that featured several of the Museum's quilts.

My interest was immediate and we began to talk in earnest. After all, 1986 was the year in which the Statue of Liberty Centennial was to be celebrated, and in time

our ongoing plans led to various meetings with Nancy Sureck, Director of Special and Cultural Events, and Beverly Siegel, Special Events Coordinator, of The Statue of Liberty, Ellis Island Foundation, Inc. The venerable lady in New York Harbor, the greatest American icon, might well serve as the national focal point for a quilt contest and subsequent national quilt festival. My desire was to use the project to enhance the popularity of the American quilt, and to make countless new friends for the Museum.

I then spoke with Nancy Lindenmeyer, Sr., Editor of Magazine Development for *Better Homes and Gardens*. Through her help the grass-roots interest in American quiltmaking became apparent. In a letter to me she stated, "...Patchwork and quilting are always among the highest testing subjects...for *Better Homes and Gardens* in the crafts area"..."One of the major sources of our research is the Yankelovich Monitor. Figures for 1983 show that in terms of sources of creativity, quiltmaking involved several million people. This, of course, does not tap the interest and appreciation of quilts as prized possessions for home accessories." "...It is my experience that nothing brings in the crowds like quilts!" Now we were certain we were on the right track.

Bruce Marsh and Jan Norton from Burson-Marsteller

and others officially approached Scotchgard® and finally a meeting was held with Nick Hilt, Brand Manager, 3M Household Products Division; Don Pirner, Brand Group Manager, 3M Household Products Division; Judith Borowski, Public Relations Representative; and with others. Gerard Wertkin, Assistant Director of the Museum of American Folk Art; Diane Finore, Curator of Special Projects; Charles Salamey, Comptroller; Lillian Grossman, my assistant; and numerous staff members ultimately joined with me and the Scotchgard® officials and everyone agreed what a splendid project this was: "The Great American Quilt Contest and Festival, A Museum of American Folk Art Event presented by Scotchgard® brand products in celebration of the Statue of Liberty Centennial"

Contracts were written and formal planning began in earnest. Sandy Smith of Sanford L. Smith & Associates, Ltd., creator of the Fall Antiques Show, was retained by the Museum to produce the Quilt Festival. Diane Finore, Curator of Special Projects, ultimately moved from the Museum staff to the Smith office where she continued to bring her special skills to the project.

Dennis Duke of Atlanta was persuaded to leave the travel business and to assume the directorship of the Festival. He has expertly coordinated every aspect of the project from the development of the biggest projects down to the smallest details.

About the same time, Donna Wilder, Director of Retail Marketing at the Fairfield Processing Corporation, became involved. What a grand day that was for the Museum! Her complete understanding of the contemporary quilters' world, of the many personalities who are the major forces in the field, and her incredible generosity have made it possible for our staff to avoid most of the difficult situations that can arise when such a complex project is undertaken.

I began to travel across the country to make a series of guest appearances on television and to hold local press conferences in an effort to inform all American quilters about the contest.

In time Donna Wilder suggested that we meet with Mary Colucci, Director of the National Needlework Association, and Leonard Ennis, Executive Vice President of the American Home Sewing Association. Both organizations assisted substantially by informing quiltmakers of our project. In fact, Mary Colucci became so interested that she agreed to coordinate "From Sea to Shining Sea," one of the major exhibits at the Festival.

Karey Bresenhan, organizer of Quilt Market and Quilt Festival and owner of Great Expectations Quilts; Bonnie Leman, Editor of Leman Publications, Inc., publishers of *Quilter's Newsletter Magazine*, and Luella Doss of Raspberry Hill Patchworks and promoter of Buttermilk Country have been of special assistance. Their generosity in the sharing of advice and their personal friendship saved us from many obstacles along the way. Tara Gillani from the New York office of Burson-Marsteller, and Susan Flamm, our Director of Public Relations, arranged for a national press conference. Nearly one hundred editors from almost every major shelter magazine and newspaper in the country were so fascinated by the project that they published numerous articles and feature stories about it. Quilters everywhere now knew about the contest, and they began to work in earnest on their entries, which would be entered in competition for the $20,000 first prize and $7,500 second prize in The Great American Quilt Contest. We also decided to select a runner-up from each state. Scotchgard® provided the funds for us to hang not only the prize-winning quilts but also the state winners. All of those quilts are illustrated in the second section of this book called "Expressions of Liberty." The quilts were selected for the exhibition by regional panels of judges, including quiltmakers, art historians, quilt- and craft-magazine editors, and museum curators. Serving on the regional panels were:

New England: Virginia Avery, Hazel Carter, Jane Hutchins

Mid Atlantic: Laurel Horton, Erma Kirkpatrick, Ruth Roberson

Southern Seaboard: Dixie Haywood, Mildred Locke, Marge Murphy

Upper Midwest: Patricia Cox, Luella Doss, Donna Hamilton

Lower Midwest: Mary Barton, Cuesta Benberry, Carla Hassel

Mountain States: Laurene Sinema, Jean DuBois, Judy Martin

West Coast: Mary Cross, Sandi Fox

Final judging was done by Karey Bresenhan, Sandi Fox, Jeff Gutcheon, Jonathan Holstein, Carter Houck, Bonnie Leman, David Pottinger, and Donna Wilder.

Fine design, expert craftsmanship, and adherence to the contest theme—"Liberty, Freedom and American

Heritage in honor of the Statue of Liberty Centennial celebration"—were among the criteria used for the selection of the national winners. Above all, the judges sought a complete work of textile art. The Contest, the Festival and the Museum rejoice in and are honored by the beauty of the quilts submitted for this great event in the quilting world.

On the following pages Dennis Duke, his Associate Project Director, Karla Friedlich, and his administrative assistant, Shirley Seglin, and I have prepared a summary of the many exhibitions, the special events, and the many educational activities that made The Great American Quilt Festival a cornerstone in increasing the interest of Americans in their great textile heritage.

Special exhibitions at The Great American Quilt Festival provided a unique opportunity to showcase some of the Museum's collections for the first time.

The presentation "Made in the U.S.A." sponsored by J. C. Penney Company, Inc., and subsequently toured nationally by the same firm included many examples of America's textile heritage assembled by Elizabeth Warren, the Museum's curator. It featured many beautiful quilts given to and purchased by the Museum. The most recent additions are the extraordinary Flag Quilt acquired with funds from the Amicus Foundation, Anne Baxter Klee, and trustees of the Museum of American Folk Art, which is illustrated on the front of this book; the splendid Baltimore Album Quilt top, a recent gift from Mr. and Mrs. James O. Keene; and several Crazy quilts, part of a most generous gift, "The Margaret Cavigga Quilt Collection" at the Museum of American Folk Art.

The thirty Amish quilts in "Continuity and Change" represent the principal areas of Amish quiltmaking: Lancaster and Mifflin counties in Pennsylvania, and Indiana and Ohio in the Midwest. Curated by Elizabeth Warren, this show documented some of the most generous contributions to the Museum's quilt collection. In June 1983, David Pottinger curated the Museum's exhibition, "Quilts from the Indiana Amish: A Regional Collection," and published his book of the same name in association with our institution, and then gave over 100 midwestern Amish quilts to our Museum. Dede and William Wigton enhanced this collection in 1984 by presenting the Museum with twenty-two very fine Amish quilts. Both the Pottinger and Wigton bedcovers greatly strengthened the focus of the quilt collection, which has frequently been enhanced by major gifts from the well-known collector and dealer Phyllis Haders. Today our

Amish quilts represent the strongest gathering of such material in any public collection.

The "Small Sensations" exhibit included doll quilts, dolls, doll furniture, miniature quilts, and sewing birds and thimbles selected by Sharon Eisenstat from many collections around the country. Of special interest were the nineteenth-century sewing birds and thimbles lent by Margaret Cavigga, and a small group of handmade dolls from nearly 150 given to the Museum by Ann Baxter Klee in memory of her mother. This exhibit was made possible by generous funding from Judi Boisson Quilts, Inc., of Southampton, New York, Westport, Connecticut, and New York City.

"The Quilts Fantastic" celebrated the interest of several of America's leading folk artists, modern artists, and Hollywood and Broadway stars in the quilting tradition. Folk artists designed quilt blocks which were executed by Lupe Miller. Denyse Montegut and Madeleine Appell stitched the quilt blocks designed by many of our nation's most famous contemporary artists. The Orange County Quilters from California fashioned the inventive designs created by such movie stars as Joan Collins, Linda Evans, Rock Hudson, Ann-Margret, Burt Reynolds, Joan Rivers, Barbra Streisand, and Elizabeth Taylor into a rich tapestry, and the Long Island Quilters of New York stitched the popular Show Quilt that depicts scenes from some of the most popular Broadway shows in recent years.

The Friends of the Museum also participated in a quilting project. A handsome design developed by Kennetha Stewart and executed by the Friends Committee, chaired this year by Cecelia Toth and Jane Walentas, featured the famous Gabriel weathervane from the Museum's collection.

The designs for the "Laura Ashley Quilts" were obtained through a national contest in which children between the ages of six and ten submitted sketches. The eight textiles produced from the designs attest to the rich inventiveness of young people in our country.

"So Proudly We Hail" was conceived and coordinated by Donna Wilder. This tribute to the history of each state through quilted flags designed and executed by fifty selected quilting guilds offered a bird's-eye view of national creativity in the quilt field. Many of the pieces featured state seals, flowers, and animals. The flags provided a colorful background to the "Wearable Art Fashion Show."

The project called "From Sea to Shining Sea" produced a continuous quilted banner measuring over

1000 feet that depicted the theme of Liberty, Freedom, and Heritage as seen by quilting members of The National Needlework Association. Mary Colucci, Director, worked with members of the organization to create panels illustrating scenes from many regions. The needlework banner began with a representation of the Statue of Liberty in New York Harbor and finished with a panel showing the Golden Gate Bridge in San Francisco.

Special events at The Great American Quilt Festival offered the opportunity to involve many people who might not otherwise have participated. The Wearable Art Fashion Show conceived by Donna Wilder and sponsored by the Fairfield Processing Corporation opened the Festival. Nearly fifty high-style, star-spangled formal and casual garments designed by many of America's finest fiber artists were modeled by several former winners of the Miss America Pageant, showing how quiltmakers have expanded their interests to include areas outside of traditional quiltmaking.

The Hawaiian Celebration, a traditional luau hosted by Jean Ariyoshi, First Lady of Hawaii, brought strong attention to the Hawaiian quilt traditions that first developed when missionaries from New England arrived in Hawaii in the 1830s and taught quilting to Hawaiian women. Enthusiasm for bold appliqué quilts with remarkable contour stitching evolved, and even today many Hawaiians continue to create beautiful bedcovers with the remarkable designs first developed over 100 years ago. The Hawaiian Celebration was chaired by Sandra Duckworth and co-chaired by Verna Kuyper. Special friends Barbara Mills and Jimmy Kaina of the Hawaiian Tourist Bureau and Elaine Zinn, Executive Director, Arts Council of Hawaii, worked tirelessly to add distinction to the event. Mealii Kalama, winner of a National Heritage Fellowship awarded by the Folk Arts Program of the National Endowment for the Arts, demonstrated her very special skills in Hawaiian quiltmaking. General Telephone and Electronics and other sponsors provided the funds for the luau, which included traditional Hawaiian foods, dancing, and breathtaking floral arrangements from Verna Kuyper's Hunalani Farm at Kiela, Maui.

Demonstrations by traditional Hmong, Amish, and Seminole quiltmakers offered a rare opportunity for visitors to the Festival to see how several ethnic and social groups developed unique quilting traditions in their own communities.

The Hmong immigrants from Southeast Asia have long worn pieced and appliquéd garments in their native land. Large immigrant communities established in recent years by refugees in New York, Iowa, Michigan, Minnesota, and other states have provided local needleworkers with new design ideas and innovative appliqué quilting techniques.

The Amish quilting traditions, tied so closely to the religious and social customs of this group, produced a unique quilting aesthetic. Amish quilters demonstrated their skills at the Festival in an Amish quilting bee.

The Seminole Indians from Florida during the nineteenth century developed a quilting tradition that was used primarily to make clothing. Stitched and pieced shirts, blouses, and skirts fashioned by Seminoles at the Quilt Festival provided firsthand knowledge about this type of American needlework to many who were totally unaware of this handsome craft.

At the Quilt Festival seventy well-known quilting experts gave courses for those who wished to perfect their designing and quiltmaking abilities.

Enrichment lectures ranged from presentations by museum curators, conservationists, collectors, and other experts. Fifteen of America's most distinguished leaders and scholars in the field shared their knowledge. Patsy Orlofsky of the Textile Conservation Center and Pat Yamin of "Come Quilt With Me" answered such practical questions as "How do I hang my quilt? What do I do about cleaning a fragile antique quilt," and Karen Berkenfeld offered advice in her presentation, "How to Solve Your Most Difficult Quilting Problems."

We are indebted to the many quilt dealers and exhibitors who displayed antique and modern quilts and quilting supplies for the quiltmaker. Their participation in the Festival was important and much appreciated by all.

Bonnie Leman, editor of *Quilter's Newsletter Magazine*; Carter Houck, editor of *Lady's Circle Patchwork Quilts*; Aloyse Yorko, editor of *Quilt*; Sandra Hatch, editor of *Stitch 'N Sew Quilts*; Barbara Hall Peterson, editor of *Quiltworld*; and the editors of *Quilters' Journal* and *The American Quilter* all deserve our thanks for their contributions to the Quilt Festival. Through their publications information about the event went out to a vast audience of collectors and quiltmakers.

A special thank you is also due Barbara Bush, National Chairwoman of The Great American Quilt Festival, and Edward I. Koch, Mayor of New York City, for the many ways in which they contributed to the event.

The Great American Quilt Contest and Festival was a

major catalyst in renewing appreciation for our national textile heritage. What a fitting legacy for future generations, for they will know that the needlework arts were an alive, vital, and beautiful part of the twentieth century. They will also know how much each American treasures the religious, political, and social freedoms that we enjoy in this great country. I can think of no better way to salute the Statue of Liberty on her 100th birthday than this offering in her honor that included participants from all over the world.

ROBERT BISHOP
Director
Museum of American Folk Art
New York City

6

ALL FLAGS FLYING

Generations of Americans were brought up on two stories about the founders of our nation: the one about George Washington, his hatchet, and the cherry tree and the other about Betsy Ross making our first flag. Both stories have been somewhat discredited. Whether or not Betsy Ross made the first flag, there were many other women who combined their skill at needlework with their patriotic feelings. Quilters especially have worked their joy, anger, sympathy, and political preferences into exciting and often artistically original pieces. Some of these were made to cover beds, but it is possible that many were made simply to be admired or made as gifts to heroes both great and unsung.

The trends in patriotic and political quilts changed with the changing styles in household textiles in general. The fabrics range from coarse homespun to the finest chintz to copperplate prints on commemorative handkerchiefs. The Victorian era brought forth a wave of elegant, if somewhat useless, silk-and-velvet quilts or "throws," often embellished with commemorative ribbons, photographs of great men, and other bits of memorabilia. During the Centennial the dates 1776–1876 were worked between the flowers and polka dots on many calico prints.

There seem to have been waves of patriotism at certain times or specific themes that appealed to quilters. In much the same way that today's trends develop, one quilter possibly used a design or an unusual fabric, and her friend or neighbor was inspired to change or improve upon the theme. There were outbursts of eagles, more or less copied from the Great Seal of the United States. Although the seal was designed in the last quarter of the eighteenth century, it took about twenty-five years for it to become a common quilt embellishment and so, perhaps spurred by the War of 1812 and the westward expansion, it occurs on many quilts in the first half of the nineteenth century.

In many cases the eagle patterns are so similar that it seems possible that a commercial version existed. In other cases designs are so obviously drawn by a none-too-skilled hand that one quilt enthusiast remarked about an early Great Seal eagle that it looked more like "a turkey on a platter." At the time of the Centennial there was a new outburst of eagles, quite different from the early ones but so similar to each other in both body style and placement on the quilts that there must at least have been a pattern that was passed around among a group of women, if not actually published.

Some political movements obviously inspired women, or at least quilters, more than others. The Whig

Party which lasted only two short decades, until the election of 1852, must have had enormous appeal. From it came patterns such as The Whig Rose, Clay's Choice, and finally Whig's Defeat. Henry Clay, who spearheaded the new party under the Whig name in opposition to Andrew Jackson said, "I'd rather be right than president." He was probably right more often than many of the politicians of the time, but he never made it to the presidency. He became one of the few losing candidates long and well remembered, at least in small part because the quilters of the time memorialized both him and his party.

The Civil War touched every household in America, and the quilters expressed their feelings with needle and thread. Some made quilts to send to their own young heroes, others to raise money or to honor the generals and leaders of the two divided governments. Eagles appeared then as symbols of the Union, and flags of both kinds blossomed on quilts from the North and South. For some years after the war the heroes' names and faces were worked into varous styles of quilts, especially the Victorian Crazy quilts of the last years of the nineteenth century.

Many presidents or candidates appear in one form or another, most often in commemorative prints, in quilts that must have been made more as political statements than as bedcoverings. In the twentieth century this mixture of the quilter's art and the political statement died down until the Great Depression and Franklin D. Roosevelt, as savior, fired the imagination of American women. There was a renaissance of quilting of all kinds in the 1930s, with patterns appearing in newspapers and magazines, quilt shows at schools and churches, and with county and state fair competitions at their height. Several books on quilts were published during this period and the first well-known quilt collectors had a heyday. The names of Carrie Hall, Rose Kretsinger, Ruth Finley, Marguerite Ickis, and Florence Peto still command respect from quilters and collectors as being the people who linked the needle arts of the nineteenth and twentieth centuries.

In the Great Depression Eleanor Roosevelt's efforts on behalf of American arts and crafts gave all women's arts new impetus, and even the WPA (Works Progress Administration) funded some special quilt projects. New designs were appearing and women were again using fabric as an art medium to create what amounted to huge posters declaring their feelings about the Depression, the administration, and finally World War II.

The time-tested idea of making a quilt as a fund-raiser helped to buy at least one bomber "for our boys."

When World War II ended, women had started along the first steps to careers outside the home, and for a while needlework fell out of favor. The baby boom, large families, and expectations of a higher scale of living drove many women back to the sewing machine in the 1950s and 1960s—if only to make clothes for themselves and their teenage daughters. Perhaps it was a desire to do something more artistic with needle and thread that brought about a new interest in quilts as a way of celebrating the Bicentennial, or perhaps it was nostalgia for the time of the Centennial, years that certainly seemed simpler to the women of 1976.

There are even those who believe that the quilt revival of the 1970s and 1980s is closely linked with the women's movement. Certainly, when politically conscious women use needle and thread to express their sentiments about government and leaders and war and peace, they are taking a stand on subjects of world importance in a time-honored feminine way. Perhaps the quilters have finally made their mark as artists in this last decade—at least more men have joined their ranks as admirers, collectors, dealers, and even quilters.

It is interesting to consider a quilt as an object of art, viewing the materials, the techniques, and the driving force behind the artist. A quilt is not something that one dreams up on a Saturday morning and completes by Sunday night, as one might a small painting or a simple piece of pottery. In terms of hours expended it is more on the order of creating a marble statue or painting a fresco. Viewed in this light, it seems almost ridiculous that one person often undertakes such a task in addition to running a household or holding an eight-hour-a-day job, or both.

For those who have sewed very little, a look at the techniques might make the labor of a quilt more understandable. For the most part they are simple techniques, basic stitches, and sewing arts as old as time. It is the perfecting of these stitches and the handling of the many pieces of fabric that separate the amateurs from the artists. A century or more ago young girls were taught from the age of four or five to use a needle, to wear a tiny thimble, and to handle scissors with care. A child of six or eight often started her first quilt, laboriously ripping out the stitches deemed too clumsy to remain in the finished article. Today's child rarely has this opportunity and often must learn at age twenty or thirty or forty to do something that would have long since been mastered by her grandmother or great-grandmother at the same age. It is considerably more difficult to make a thimble and needle perform exactly as you wish when you start late in life, but the challenge is compelling enough to make many people overcome the obstacles.

The basic stitches are of two kinds, the easiest being the running stitch used for piecing and for quilting the layers together. It is almost always the first stitch learned, if for nothing more than to mend the seams of a skirt, shirt, or pants. The hard part is to get the stitches so even that they hold the tiny seams of a pieced quilt without gap or flaw. It is even more difficult to make them perform with grace and ease as they run along the surface of a quilt, holding the top, batting, and backing together. They should, at best, become a part of the decoration of the quilt surface, and woe unto the needler who leaves knots showing on the back or front!

The blind stitch for appliqué should be just that—totally invisible or blind! It requires somewhat more practice than the running stitch, but little girls in the eighteenth and nineteenth centuries learned it at an early stage. Many of the elegant appliqués of the *Broderie Perse* type, in which entire motifs were cut from chintz prints and were applied to another fabric surface, were held down with fine embroidery stitches, adding texture to the surface and a strong definition to the edge of each motif. Fine threads, sometimes silk, and sometimes highly polished or mercerized cotton, and a buttonhole or herringbone stitch were the usual choices for this surface decoration. As you look at the old quilts, and especially at these elaborate commemorative pieces, you will recognize several other embroidery stitches used in the signatures, in architectural details, and in the fine lines of faces in the portraits.

The Victorian era brought together all the techniques of quilting and of fine needlework. There was open competition to see how many embroidery stitches could be used in one silk-and-velvet Crazy quilt. Piecing, appliqué, embroidery, and even painting and photographic printing on fabric were incorporated into these marvelous confections. They were strictly for show—"throws" to be used on the end of the horsehair sofa—not bedcovers. Politicians and heroes found their way into the fabric of Victoriana along with ribbons from a variety of fairs, celebrations, and firemen's balls.

Even if one knows how a quilt is made, there remains the question of why—what is the motivation? Florence Peto, one of the great quilt collectors of the mid-twentieth century, was also a lecturer and writer on the subject, and finally a quilter. She had always been an expert needlewoman but had made only one quilt, as many women do, for her daughter. She not only collected quilts but also stockpiled wonderful antique fabrics. It was inevitable that she would be tempted to try her hand—and with what better than these antique pieces of cloth, printed not only in florals but in patriotic themes? The results are delicate and lovely pieces spanning a century from fabric to finished product.

Often a piece of fabric, be it old or new, will be the catalyst that drives a quilter to design something special and beautiful. The resplendent album quilts with their wreaths of flowers and bowls of fruit, often serve to preserve pieces of elegant chintz, cut out, elaborately rearranged, and stitched, *Broderie Perse* style, to a solid background. The fabric itself must have suggested the final quilt. Certainly the commemorative prints of presidents, maps, historic buildings, and battles lured the quilter to plan and frame and combine with other fabrics to make a lasting hymn of praise to a historic event or time.

The desire of a craftsman or woman to execute some intricate piece of work is often almost like an ache in the fingers or in the mind. It is like having a recurring melody going around and around in the head until it must come out through the fingers on the keys of a piano. Designers during the Bicentennial began to get ideas in their heads and longed to put them together in proper order to express something they felt about America. Sometimes they enlisted several other people or were themselves enlisted by a group so that their design could be more quickly executed by several quilters working together. The results of many of these group efforts will probably hang in town halls, libraries, museums, and state buildings for the enjoyment of all visitors at least until the Tricentennial, when there may well be a whole new explosion of commemorative quilts.

We cannot know exactly what spurred our grandmothers and great-grandmothers long ago to make their patriotic quilts, but we do have very definite accounts by women who created Bicentennial quilts. Gladys Boalt, who spearheaded the creation of the beautiful *Putnam Valley Quilt* (fig. 55), has written the history of that joint endeavor, which we have excerpted here.

The Putnam County Quilt has been a source of pride and joy, love, and inspiration to those who made it as well as those who gaze upon it. The overwhelming abundance of historical material gave us the chance to design a quilt that would not only be historically interesting and correct but beautiful and different from the multitude of block-by-block quilts that were being made at the same time.

It began as a dream to a few women who wanted to make a quilt to commemorate Putnam County, New York, during the Bicentennial celebration in 1976. Many times during the course of this endeavor we had problems in both the quilting and the personal relations. We all came through it in good spirit—perhaps it is the nature of women to work well together most of the time. We were all good friends when we started and we still are.

One member of the group, when she saw the project, proclaimed: "No one's going to get me to take perfectly good fabric, cut it into little pieces and sew it back together again!" Fortunately for us she was an artist and when she became convinced that appliqué was painting with fabric, she caved in and created three parts to the quilt, all masterpieces. Another member had never sewn anything more than a button on her husband's shirt but became an apt and willing student and completed a stunning mill in appliqué.

Some did more work than others. My mother-in-law, Anne Boalt, did several sections and most of the setting together and quilting. We truly could not have done it without her steadfast hand. Each person who worked on the quilt was proud of her own accomplishment, small or large. It became a source of fulfillment to all.

We had many difficult moments that caused chagrin or worry. After working months to complete and set in place an absolutely correct picture of the county courthouse, the county officials of the time decided to paint the building another color. We decided, in order to prevent the appliqué artist from having a nervous breakdown, we'd just leave ours as it had been made.

We searched for weeks for pictures of landmarks long gone and people long dead. One thing we simply could not find was a portrait of General Israel Putnam. We were turned down by libraries and historical societies alike. One day I was casually glancing through an old historical magazine that had been on my shelf for years. I was looking for American soldiers in uniform when my eyes fell on a full page lithograph of the crusty old general in full regalia and on horseback. My screams of delight brought my husband running!

It is such a few years since we made that Bicentennial quilt and yet many of us look back and say, "How did we find time to do it?" Whenever it is shown we are both proud and humbled to see women sometimes stand in front of it with tears in their eyes. These people tell us over and over that they are grateful to us for making the Putnam County Quilt. Is it the history of our nation that stirs them? Is it the loving hands that sewed it, or is it the beauty of it? We don't really know, but each time it happens we are certain that it was a brave endeavor and a fulfilling one and that the nineteen women who labored to give it birth are mighty proud of it.

Women like Jean Mitchell of Kansas and Mary Pemble Barton of Iowa worked alone on their Bicentennial quilts, putting time and thought and love and a wonderful sense of design into them. Each one worked in a Medallion style, with a distinct center section and surrounding borders. They chose from history, from family records, and from memory the things that pleased them and that would later please the people who saw the quilts. Each one pieced together her picture of America in fabrics and traditional quilt designs, and figures of the people, and the eagle, that great symbol of the United States.

The center of Mary Pemble Barton's quilt stands for God and country, with the eagle and the churches. She cut the eagle from a drapery fabric, *Broderie Perse* style, adding the arrows and olive branch and shield. The small simple churches stand for all of the spired houses of worship, large and small, across the country. She said that her first ideas were too overwhelming and she found it necessary to simplify in deference to her fabric medium.

Like Florence Peto before her, Mary Pemble Barton collected fabrics and used some that were as much as a hundred years old. She mentions that the roofs of the houses enclosing the eagle and churches were made from apron and housedress fabrics of the late nineteenth and early twentieth centuries. The houses represent the cabins in the wilderness, in a clearing between the pine trees. It is interesting that both Jean Mitchell and Mary Pemble Barton used that early American quilt block, the Pine Tree, in their commemorative quilts.

For many viewers of Mary's quilt the women stand

out as the most interesting feature. She says of them, "The three parts of each were cut alike but in the appliqué process they took on different postures and sizes. Each woman wears a different print—fabrics typical of the working class. They walk like ladies, giving elegance to the many indigo-blue fabrics. It's uncanny to me how happy they seem to look. Their walk is one of hope and adventure. The woman in black is my recognition of death and hardships during the [westward] migration."

Mary explains that each miniature quilt block in the women's path is different, and one stands for the Civil War, her only mention of wars in the entire quilt. Mary says of the message: "My feelings or intents were towards making this a memorial to unsung generations of people striving to have better lives and land for their children. My imagination tells me that they picked up quilt ideas from others on the wagon train and that they had pleasant thoughts of quilts, tops and blocks made to take west, and that they dreamed of those quilts to be made when they reached their destination. We aren't reminded of the hours that will be spent preparing food, making clothing, and making a house a home in their new location."

Mary's own family and bits of her childhood are subtly remembered. She says that the men wear suspenders because the family records have it that her own great-grandpa Lisle bought his first ones just before he married Mary Evans in 1839. She goes on to say that she considers him quite typical of the settlers. The men all carry building and farming tools and walk along a background of Rail Fence piecing.

A dress Mary wore in her childhood is remembered near the copyright in the lower left corner. She says, "The dress was made by Ruth Miller whose sisters were the well-known quilters of California, Christine and Hortense Miller. They formerly lived in my hometown."

In the same corner is carefully inscribed a quotation from a Guthrie County, Iowa, newspaper dated October 28, 1869: "Last spring we daily witnessed long lines of emigrant wagons passing through Panora, coming from points farther east to settle in this county or even farther west as the case may be. Of late these trains are seen again daily in no small proportions. Large trains sometimes numbering wagons by the dozen pass through, each containing a family, household goods, and extra stock suggestive of permanent settlement. Many who yet remain in the states where small results come from long toiling could do no better than to seek the fertile lands in Guthrie County."

There are also records of the families that went to make up Mary Pemble Barton's heritage, family names, dates, and countries of origin all recorded. The lines of migration are on the map in the lower right corner, extending no farther than Iowa, where her family came to settle permanently.

The more one looks the more there is to see in this gentle history lesson. On the side of one wagon is a plow. The scouts stand firmly in each corner between those long lines of women in blue. There are campfires to warm the weary travelers, and more quilt designs on wagon sides. The only bear is a friendly enough creature, standing beside a scout. Mary Pemble Barton's grandchildren and many generations to come will learn about their heritage from this intricate and beautifully designed quilt, the top having been made entirely by one imaginative woman. It was quilted by a group of women from St. Petri's Lutheran Church in Story City, Iowa.

The Bicentennial now seems a long time ago and yet the impetus given to quilting has apparently not died down. Are there new patriotic themes for people to stitch into their quilts? The people of the Idaho Peace Quilt Group think so. They have labored not only to make quilts symbolizing peace but also to bring them to the attention of the people of this and other countries, and to the leaders who have it in their power to vote for the bills that will lead us away from war. Perhaps in the future the message of all patriotic quilts will be as gentle as their enormous *Peace Quilt* designed by children and Mary Pemble Barton's *Heritage Quilt* with its lines of women in blue and men with the tools of building peace, not war. Perhaps some day in the far-distant future there will be no generals to have their names emblazoned on quilts, no wars to commemorate, and our eagle can drop the arrows from his talon.

CARTER HOUCK
Editor
Lady's Circle Patchwork Quilts

1. Coverlet, hand-blocked linen, blue-and-red patriotic pattern together with Masonic symbols and a portrait of Thomas Jefferson, c. 1800. 96″ x 77″. Very little is known about the origin of this piece, except that it was *not* made by any member of Jefferson's family, several of whom were accomplished artists and needlewomen. The sixteen stars date it to about the time of his first election to the presidency, when there were sixteen states. By 1805, when he returned to that office for his second term, Ohio had become the seventeenth state. As a candidate for office Thomas Jefferson, Virginia planter and slave owner, gave way to "Thomas Jefferson, Esq., The Man of the People." Photograph by Myron Miller. (Monticello, the Home of Thomas Jefferson)

2. Pieced, embroidered, and appliqué cotton quilt with poster-bed corners, c. 1819. 72″ x 82″. There are twenty-two stars framing the U.S. Navy eagle, probably signifying the number of states at the time the quilt was made, placing it prior to early 1820, when Maine became the twenty-third state. Some family member may have served in the navy, a hero at least to the quilter, perhaps in the War of 1812. Dyes of this early period were often unstable, so it can be assumed that the browns were of some brighter shade, or perhaps even another color. (The Shelburne Museum, Shelburne, Vermont)

3. Detail of a quilt pieced with early cotton prints and a commemorative kerchief titled *The Death of General Washington*, 1800–1810. 97½″ x 96″. Besides being historically interesting, this quilt is a compendium of late eighteenth-century textiles, quite possibly both European and American. The kerchief shows a familiar deathbed scene, complete with physician and grief-stricken widow. Framing the scene are various inscriptions concerning Washington's accomplishments and contributions to mankind, and in the circles at left and right are these special tributes: "He was GREAT in the COUNCIL and in the FIELD," and "He was GREAT in ARTS and in ARMS." This may well be the earliest-known quilt using a printed commemorative kerchief. (Collection of Mr. and Mrs. Foster McCarl, Jr.)

4. Pieced, appliqué, and *Broderie Perse* chintz on solid white cotton background, c. 1820, Connecticut. 104″ x 102″. As the eastern United States became more prosperous and houses grander, the scale of beds, quilts, and other furnishings became larger and often more elegant. This one represents the height of the needlewoman's art for the grandest of rooms. The eagle of the Great Seal is perfectly proportioned to blend with the baskets and bouquets of chintz flowers. The inner border of tiny pieced triangles and large floral outer border must have showed to great advantage hanging on the sides of a high bed. The fine cross-hatch quilting keeps the batting smooth and protects the fabric as it holds the layers firmly together. Photograph courtesy Gerald Kornblau.

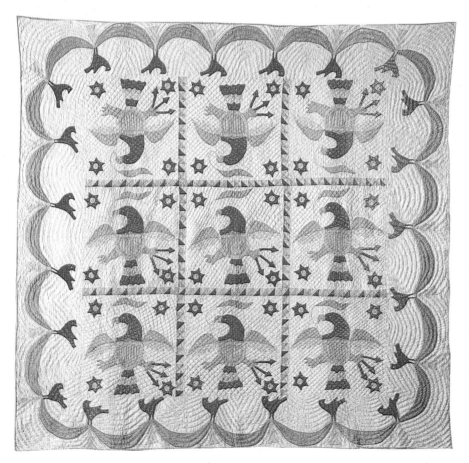

5. Pieced and appliqué cotton quilt, attributed to Lydia Stafford, first half of the nineteenth century, Vermont. 100½″ x 84″. The sprightly red, green, and yellow eagles with banners and arrows, but no olive branches, were possibly created in a burst of young and patriotic enthusiasm—or so the legend goes—for Lydia Stafford's hope chest in expectation of her marriage to Warren Barstowe on his return from the War of 1812. The one row of eagles at the left was purposely made upside down to accommodate the fall at the side of the bed, so that when seen in place no eagles would be standing on their heads. The swag border is beautifully executed with tassels and red birds in a sea of quilting. Both the eagle and the bird are so similar to ones on other quilts it seems possible that some patterns were passed around if not actually published, but none has come to light. Photograph by Ken Burris. (The Shelburne Museum)

14

6. Appliqué blue-and-white cotton print on white cotton, made by Susan Strong Bell, c. 1835, either Maryland or Ohio. 89″ x 80″. Susan Strong Bell was born in Frederick County, Maryland, and like many women of her time, moved west after her marriage to William Bell in 1831, when she was twenty-two years old. It is possible that she made this remarkably feminine version of the Great Seal of the United States either before she was married or after she settled in Ohio. Notice that the eagle holds no arrows of war, only vines and leaves, and is surrounded by vases of trailing vines and flowers. (Smithsonian Institution, Washington, D.C.)

7. Appliqué Album quilt top, c. 1840, probably Maryland. 88″ x 88″. The motifs on this quilt, undoubtedly a group or "friendship" effort, are similar to many other Baltimore Album quilts of the 1840s. There is the ubiquitous eagle, but more exciting to the searcher for political meaning is the log cabin. The 1840 campaign of William Henry Harrison and John Tyler was referred to as "log cabin and hard cider," pointing to the humble origins of the Whigs as opposed to the supposedly patrician Democrats in power. Slogans and symbols have always made better campaigns than issues, although the issue was a fairly compelling depression in 1840. The other memorable slogan was "Tippecanoe and Tyler too," referring to an 1811 victory of then General Harrison over Tecumseh. This bloody battle at Tippecanoe Creek marked, in a way, the beginning of the end—"The Trail of Tears"—for the Indians east of the Mississippi River. (Smithsonian Institution)

7a. Detail of the William Henry Harrison log cabin, complete with hard-cider barrel.

16

8. Pieced and embroidered quilt with appliqué chintz and other cotton prints and solid colors on a white background, c. 1840, Connecticut. 77″ x 75″. Star of Bethlehem quilts were very popular from 1800 to 1850—and, indeed, are again. The design allows the quilter to use her scraps to wonderful advantage and to fill the large white spaces in the sides and corners with any personal statement she wishes to make. The elegant prints in the eagles have been used to great advantage, whereas the more common solids and prints have been cut into small pieces forming the kaleidoscopic star. This quilt descended to the present day in the Keeler family of Ridgefield, Connecticut, although no one is sure of the maker's name. The eagles show a fine burst of New England patriotism and an interesting little change—a rosebud replaces the usual olive branch. In every other respect this is the familiar eagle of the Great Seal. Photograph by William Shea. (Scott-Fanton Museum, Danbury, Connecticut; gift of Marion Magelton)

9. Pieced and appliqué cotton quilt, Presidential Wreath, made in the Traver family, c. 1840, New York State. 96″ x 96″. The pattern honoring the president was designed in New Jersey about 1835. This handsome version has 25-inch blocks and finely pieced sashes and borders. It is in the vibrant red, white, and green so often used in quilts of the second quarter of the nineteenth century. The quilt stayed in the original family, being passed down to daughters; Traver, Brown, and Upton families owned it until it was acquired by the museum in 1979. (The Shelburne Museum)

10. Appliqué and embroidered cotton quilt, made by L.W., dated 1844, Pennsylvania. 75″ x 67″. The bold blue eagles hold arrows that look more like knitting needles and stiff olive branches with no olives. Although it was a feminine fashion at the time to inscribe one's name and date in mirror writing, it does seem idiosyncratic, to say the least, that the maker of this quilt went to the trouble to letter each of the five banners with *E Pluribus Unum* in reverse. She also added some rather young and gleeful birds, hearts, and new moons, and filled all the blank spaces with stars, in this case having nothing to do with the number of states in the Union. (Private collection)

18

11. Pieced cotton quilt, campaign prints and solid colors, c. 1844, probably Pennsylvania. 106″ x 96″. Considering how little most of us remember about President James K. Polk, except that he belongs to that list of one-term presidents that all schoolchildren learn to rattle off, it is interesting to think about the excitement and controversy he probably stirred up at the time of his election in 1844. He believed in expansion and the country's "manifest destiny." The one star at the right of his portrait represents Texas, which became the twenty-eighth state after his election. There are twenty-six stars in the flags, but Florida gained statehood between Polk's election and his inauguration, and Texas, the twenty-eighth, not until the end of 1845. The Mexican War erupted during his presidency, gaining for the United States the land that would become Arizona, New Mexico, and a large part of California. The records are unclear, but there is reason to believe that the city of Dallas (first settled in 1841) was named for George Mifflin Dallas, Polk's vice-president, a Pennsylvanian. The other man named in the center block is Francis R. Shunk, Governor of Pennsylvania 1844–1848. Because Shunk's name is so prominent it appears almost certain that the quilt was made in Pennsylvania. Photograph courtesy The Shelburne Museum. (White House Collection)

12. Pieced, appliqué, and embroidered cotton *Major Ringgold Quilt*, c. 1846, Maryland. 110″ x 94″. At least two Baltimore Album quilts have a Major Ringgold tomb with rifles, flags, and flowers. If he is a hero whose name does not have a familiar ring, you probably have not studied Maryland history. He was born in Washington County, Maryland, and was killed at the Battle of Palo Alto, Texas, in 1846, one of the first heroes of the Mexican War. The spiral of flowers just to the left of the tomb is signed M°OREM, possibly not an abbreviated signature but a sign or symbol of some fraternal order—the lower left corner block has several such symbols, including the all-seeing eye and the moon and stars of the International Order of Odd Fellows. The two eagles are similar to the one seen in the Harrison "Log Cabin and Hard Cider" quilt (fig. 7) and found in many other Baltimore quilts of the time. It seems somewhat strange that a quilt commemorating a fallen war hero should have eagles with no arrows in their talons, although one researcher believes that the Ringgold block was added after the quilt was completed. Photograph by Ken Burris. (The Shelburne Museum)

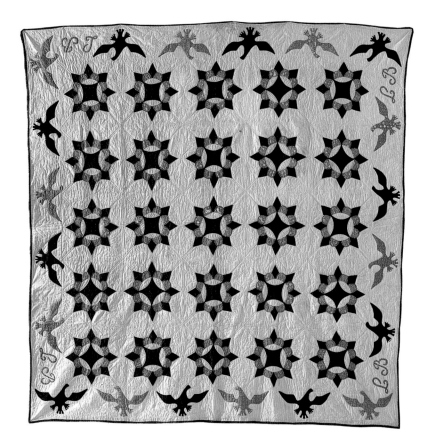

13. Pieced and appliqué cotton quilt, Caesar's Crown, c. 1850. 86″ x 83″. The eagles in the border and the lovely script initials, L.B., worked in fine appliqué, tell only a very small part of the story of this quilt. The maker was obviously patriotic enough to include eagles; did she then intend some hidden meaning in the Caesar's Crown motif? Unfortunately, the later life of this quilt is better documented than its origins. It was once in the collection of Florence Peto, one of the first of the twentieth-century quilt collectors and authorities. (Collection of Virginia Avery)

14. Appliqué cotton quilt, c. 1850, possibly Baltimore. 105″ x 104″. Like so many quilts, this one has had a some-what checkered career, from perhaps aristocratic origins to a trunk at a public auction where it was sold as an unquilted top. Catherine Gardner bought this marvelous piece and had it quilted about 1940, probably a hundred years after it was made. The eagles bear such a strong resemblance to those found in Baltimore quilts of the 1840–1850 period, which have been attributed to Mary Ann Evans, that it is believed to have made its way from that area to Kansas. Two flags containing twenty-nine stars are presumably from 1847, and the other two with thirty-one possibly date from 1851, thus saying something about how long it often takes a quilter to complete such a large piece of work. (Collection of Catherine Gardner)

15. Pieced, embroidered, and appliqué polished cotton and chintz quilt with wool yarn, c. 1850, Kentucky. 102″ x 81″. Every block of this quilt is exquisitely worked with the finest techniques. Some blocks are crewel embroidered with wool yarn. The chintz cutouts are laid down in *Broderie Perse* style, embroidered around the edge and over some of the designs to give a raised look. The fine quilting, ten to twelve stitches to the inch, was worked a block at a time, like the block-by-block quilting so popular today. The needlewoman is said to have been Lucretia Hart Clay, wife of Henry Clay whose portrait (based on an oil by John Neagle, 1842) is beautifully executed in crewel yarn in the center block. It is also believed that the quilt was made as a gift to the wife of John Jordan Crittenden, Clay's long-time friend and associate in government. The last private owner was a descendant of that family. Photograph by Tommy Hughes. (The Kentucky Museum, Western Kentucky University, Bowling Green, Kentucky)

16. Pieced, appliqué, and block-printed quilt, dated 1852, possibly New Jersey or Pennsylvania. 78″ x 78″. There was nothing so special about 1852, except in retrospect. It marked no centennial or other such time for national celebration, but it was the year of the election of a rather unremarkable one-term president, Franklin Pierce, an election marking the end of the Whig Party. It was also the year of the publication of *Uncle Tom's Cabin* by Harriet Beecher Stowe—an event that cast a long shadow over the next several decades. The maker of this quilt with its elegant combination of techniques was looking more toward the past glories than the future problems of her country. From the top, in the center of the pieced Chips and Whetstones blocks, the first thirteen presidents are listed in this odd order (reading clockwise)—neither chronological nor alphabetical: George Washington, Thomas Jefferson, James Monroe, Andrew Jackson, William Henry Harrison, Martin Van Buren, John Tyler, Zachary Taylor, Millard Fillmore, James K. Polk, John Adams, James Madison, John Quincy Adams. Many of the names are abbreviated to fit the small hexagons. (Peto Collection)

17. Pieced and appliqué quilt, Whig's Defeat, c. 1852. 79″ x 77″. The short-lived Whig Party went down to defeat in the elections of 1852, so we must surmise that its admirers invented this interesting design as a fitting memorial to it. "The Flag of the Union," as it is labeled in this quilt, contains thirty-one stars, indicating that the quilt was made after 1850, when California was admitted. There was, however, still enough interest in the Whig Party for the Henry Clay and Zachary Taylor kerchiefs to be available for inclusion in the quilt. There seems to be no absolutely clear information on the date of the first Whig's Defeat quilt being made—just before or just after the debacle of 1852? The verse inscribed below the flag reads: "As long as thy waves shall gleam in the Sun,/And long as thy Heroes remember their Scars,/Be the hands of Thy Children united as one,/And peace shed Her Light on the Banner of Stars.//Hail! Thou Republic of Washington, Hail!/Never may Star of thy Union wax pale,/Hope of the World! may each Omen of ill,/Fade in the light of thy Destiny still." (Collection of Mr. and Mrs. Foster McCarl, Jr.)

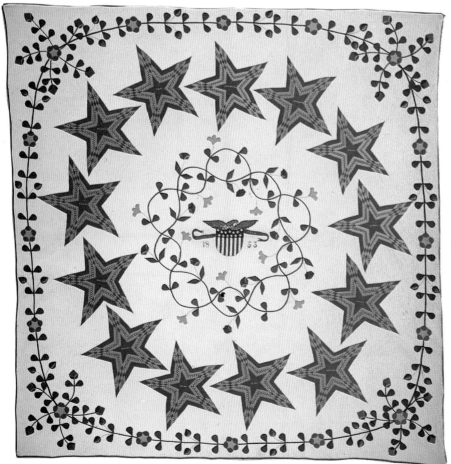

18. Pieced and appliqué quilt, dated 1853. 86¼″ x 85″. The amazing relationship between this mid-nineteenth-century quilt and the one in figure 16 is in some ways more puzzling for its differences than for its similarities. The diamond-pieced stars are not nearly so expertly made as the Chips and Whetstones blocks of the 1852 version. In this wonderfully American confection it is the thirteen Colonies, not the thirteen presidents, that take their places in the centers of the pieced stars. By this time the fourteenth president had been sworn into office, requiring another star where there does not seem to be space for any addition. We will be left with the eternal question, did one woman make these two quilts, perhaps starting this one first, losing interest, and finishing the other, or were they made for some sort of competition? The names of the thirteen original Colonies are embroidered: New Hampshire, Massachusetts, Rhode Island, Connecticut, New York, New Jersey, Delaware, Pennsylvania, Maryland, Virginia, North Carolina, South Carolina, and Georgia. (Indianapolis Museum of Art, Indianapolis, Indiana)

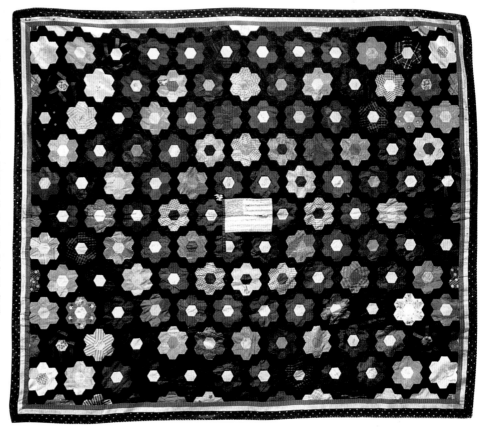

19. Pieced silk quilt, made by Mary Alice Hughes Lord, 1864, Nashville, Tennessee. 70″ x 80″. The maker of this quilt was not only able to obtain the autographs of President Lincoln and many of his U.S. Army generals, but is said also to have carried this piece with her from Tennessee through the rebel lines to Cincinnati and back again. The white areas in the flag and several of the white hexagons bear the delicately inked names. One wonders if she sent the small pieces to these illustrious gentlemen, as we now send pieces of autograph quilts to favorite movie stars, waiting anxiously for the scraps to return, perhaps through those same enemy lines, name in place and note attached. She finished the quilt in the proper Victorian style, with ribbon, cording, and tassels. (Smithsonian Institution; gift of the maker's children: Rose H. and William Craige Lord)

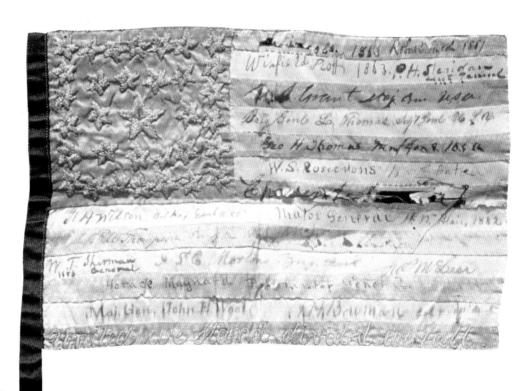

19a. Detail of the center section of the Civil War autograph quilt.

20. Appliqué and pieced-cotton *Nunda Lodge Quilt*, 1865, McHenry County, Illinois. 82″ x 82″. The sheer patriotic enthusiasm of this quilt almost diverts the viewer's attention from the intricacies of the design and workmanship. The maker or makers certainly got everything in it that held meaning for them and for many other people at this end-of-the-war era. There is no doubt of the Union sympathies and who the heroes were! "Pure Water" may have been a reference to the Temperance Movement, ever present in the last half of the nineteenth century. (Chicago Historical Society, Chicago, Illinois)

21. Pieced, appliqué, and embroidered cotton summer quilt, c. 1865. 83½″ x 78″. This quilt was undoubtedly made by several people as a friendship or presentation piece, perhaps for a bride or a local minister. There are many personal references—pets, a house, and so forth—and two political blocks, both depicting Lincoln. The one in the upper right is well done and highly recognizable. The one at the left edge, center row, is Lincoln (very tall and top-hatted) in debate with Stephen A. Douglas (short and hot-tempered). There are signatures and dates, but there is nothing that gives a definite clue to the exact locale, except that it was probably a rural area. Photograph by Ken Burris. (The Shelburne Museum)

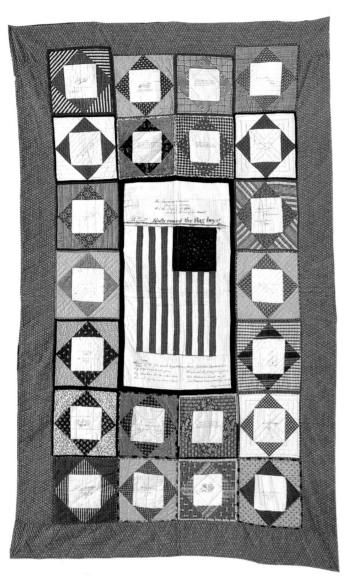

22. Pieced cotton quilt with inked inscriptions, 1865, Florence, Massachusetts. 85″ x 53″. Certainly a mother, aunt, sister, or fiancée must have lovingly made this quilt to fit the cot of a soldier boy in blue. It was apparently never used. We can hope that this was because the war ended and he treasured it forever, but it is just possible that the sayings so carefully penned on it were not as pleasing to the ears of a young man as to the women in his life. These are samples of the kindly meant and moral lines: "Ye are Martyrs in a good cause."/"Be true to humanity and to freedom."/"Touch not intoxicating drinks."/"Quiet Conscience gives quiet sleep."/"Touch not Tobacco—a curse on it."//"REBELS: They mock our peaceful labor/ They scorn our useful toil/ But on their vain pretensions/ The blow will surely fall!" This quilt may even have been a group effort with each of the friends and relatives turning in a block. (America Hurrah Antiques, N.Y.C.)

23. Pieced and appliqué quilt, third quarter of the nineteenth century, New Jersey. 112″ x 96″. Oral tradition has it that this quilt was made late in the Civil War by a wounded and discharged veteran. The quilt was passed down in his family in New Jersey, the story with it. Some of the fine fabrics can be dated to the earlier part of the nineteenth century, so it may be assumed that he came from a family that sewed and made quilts and that someone—wife, mother, or sister—started him on his project as occupational therapy. There are very explicitly warlike figures in the center and one border. The center also contains some things we might call "a soldier's dreams." There are doves, perhaps signifying peace, hearts, and ladies bearing trays. These last seem very similar to a trademark (from the year 1780) for a fine brand of chocolate. Photograph by Ken Burris. (The Shelburne Museum)

24. Appliqué and embroidered cotton quilt, 1860–1880. 73″ x 66″. Many of the symbols in this quilt are political, as are some of the figures. The ship *Constitution* is easily recognizable in the center. It is flanked by two of the familiar eagle blocks on the left and on the right. The block next to the eagle on the right has some fraternal-order symbols. There are two men in Union uniforms in the lower section, and a portrait and a statue of two other men in the upper portion. These may all have been easily identifiable at the time the quilt was created. The biblical references are clear: Adam and Eve, Abraham and Isaac, David with his harp, Cain and Abel, and a lion and a lamb, to mention a few. A complete symbolic chart of this quilt might well prove to be a key to the maker or makers and the period in which they lived. (America Hurrah Antiques, N.Y.C.)

25. Pieced cotton quilt containing printed Centennial kerchiefs, made by Esther Elizabeth Cooley, 1876, Massachusetts. 73″ x 76½″. Any woman returning home from the great Centennial Exposition in Philadelphia would probably have brought back with her a few of the popular printed kerchiefs sold there in great numbers. Esther Cooley seems to have planned her purchase well enough to make a properly balanced quilt design with a center proclaiming the wonders of Fairmount Park, Philadelphia. Her kerchiefs differ from the ones in the quilt in figure 26, but the spirit of 1876 is rampant in both. (Smithsonian Institution)

25a. Close-up of the center kerchief in the Cooley Centennial quilt, showing Fairmount Park in Philadelphia.

26.   Pieced cotton quilt of printed Centennial kerchiefs, c. 1876. 104″ x 83″. The Philadelphia Centennial Exposition must have been an unqualified success—at least to the merchants who printed and sold commemorative cotton squares or kerchiefs, judging by the number of them that have survived to this day. The various kerchiefs in this quilt represent such memorable themes as the Declaration of Independence, George Washington (also found in several repeat borders), The Memorial Hall Art Gallery in Philadelphia, and the flags and coats of arms of participating nations. The blue background with white stars and the 1776 and 1876 dates round out the thoroughly patriotic theme. Photograph courtesy Phyllis and Sydney Rosner. (Judith Pedersen and John McElhatton)

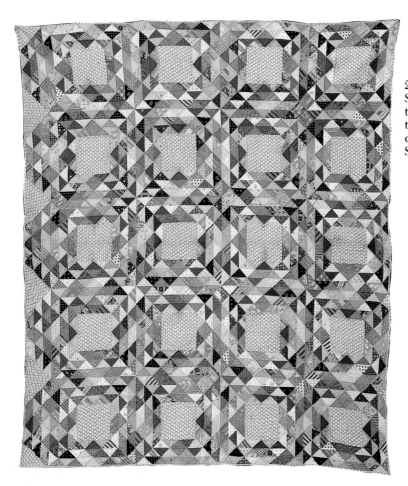

27. Pieced cotton quilt, Ocean Waves, 1876, New York State. 80″ x 68″. At first glance it is hard to determine that this attractive quilt of traditional design has a patriotic theme. Only with a close look can the Centennial prints dated 1776–1876 be detected. (Collection of Joyce Schlotzhauer)

27a. Detail of the Ocean Waves quilt showing Centennial prints at top and left.

28. Pieced cotton quilt of printed Centennial kerchiefs and commemorative textiles, late nineteenth century. 89″ x 94″. The familiar outlines of Memorial Hall in Philadelphia dominate this star-studded quilt. Some of the prints are identical to those in figures 25 and 26, and seem to be kerchiefs. The remainder, with flags, coats of arms, and so forth, seem to have been cut from yard goods, judging by the printed borders. Not one of these quilts is truly exquisite as a piece of textile art, but the outburst of patriotism in which they were created is certainly an interesting phenomenon of the last quarter of the nineteenth century, when Americans were realizing their power and potential. (The Shelburne Museum)

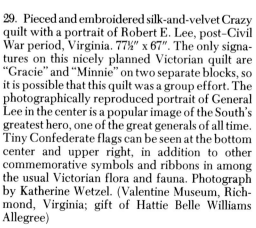

29. Pieced and embroidered silk-and-velvet Crazy quilt with a portrait of Robert E. Lee, post–Civil War period, Virginia. 77½″ x 67″. The only signatures on this nicely planned Victorian quilt are "Gracie" and "Minnie" on two separate blocks, so it is possible that this quilt was a group effort. The photographically reproduced portrait of General Lee in the center is a popular image of the South's greatest hero, one of the great generals of all time. Tiny Confederate flags can be seen at the bottom center and upper right, in addition to other commemorative symbols and ribbons in among the usual Victorian flora and fauna. Photograph by Katherine Wetzel. (Valentine Museum, Richmond, Virginia; gift of Hattie Belle Williams Allegree)

30. Appliqué cotton quilt, origin unknown, last quarter of the nineteenth century. 82″ x 82″. So many of these "fat eagles" appeared on quilts in the late nineteenth century, probably after the Centennial celebrations, that it is almost certain there was a pattern for them. It is interesting to compare this one to the one at the Abby Aldrich Rockefeller Folk Art Center, Williamsburg, Virginia, in which the eagles wear crowns and apparently smoke cigars. All of the eagles in the quilts earlier than this time seem to be much slimmer and more menacingly like the great birds of prey; these seem almost cartoonlike in their chubby charm. (America Hurrah Antiques, N.Y.C.)

31. Printed cotton quilt backing, c. 1880. 102″ x 64″. The top of this single-bed quilt is made of simple triangles and has no political significance. The printed back provides us with a look at several yards of one of those great campaign fabrics that seemed to be a staple of the quilter's scrap bag in the mid to late nineteenth century. The flags are beautifully draped and the small signs under the portraits urge the reader to vote: "James A. Garfield for President" and "Chester A. Arthur for Vice President." Garfield is remembered mostly for the fact that he was shot by a maniac shortly after he became president and lingered through a long hot summer until he died in September. Arthur was the president credited with the Pendleton Civil Service Reform Act, designed to do away with patronage. He was a slightly shoddy politician before rising unexpectedly to the land's highest office and, like at least one later such man, proved that a small man can grow fairly successfully into a large job. Photograph by Ken Burris. (The Shelburne Museum)

32. Pieced cotton quilt of scrap prints and commemorative kerchief, c. 1884, New York State. 86″ x 85″. Grover Cleveland was the first Democratic president since before the Civil War. He came into office in the election of 1884 as a bachelor and was the first president to marry in the White House. His bride was the young, attractive Frances Folsom, daughter of his deceased law partner and for some years his ward. He became the only man ever to be president in two separated terms (1885 and 1893), with the one-term Benjamin Harrison between. He ran for office all three times, winning the largest number of popular votes in all three elections but losing to Harrison in the Electoral College. For all his stout genial look, he was apparently a rather serious and very ethical man. Look at the quilt in figure 36, and you will see his Republican rival, the man who split the two terms, Benjamin Harrison. It seems quite possible that the two quilts were done by the same hand, in spite of the political differences. (Museum of American Folk Art, New York; gift of Made in America)

33. Pieced and heavily embroidered silk-and-velvet Crazy quilt with campaign ribbons, c. 1885. 61″ x 78″. The maker of this quilt was obviously a Democrat! She had backed the two Democratic losers in the race for the presidency in 1876 and 1880: Samuel Tilden (lower left corner of center panel) and Winfield Hancock (lower right corner of center panel). The flag at the top proclaims the first Democratic victory in twenty-eight years with the inauguration date (March 4, 1885) for Grover Cleveland (upper left corner of center panel) and his vice-president, Thomas A. Hendricks (upper right corner of center panel). The rooster was a common symbol in Cleveland's campaigns and the deep pink ribbon at the center top between the rooster and the flag is a joint portrait of Cleveland and Hendricks. The ribbon below the center with the two grimacing faces is evidently the work of one of the political cartoonists of the day. (Museum of American Folk Art; gift of Margaret Cavigga)

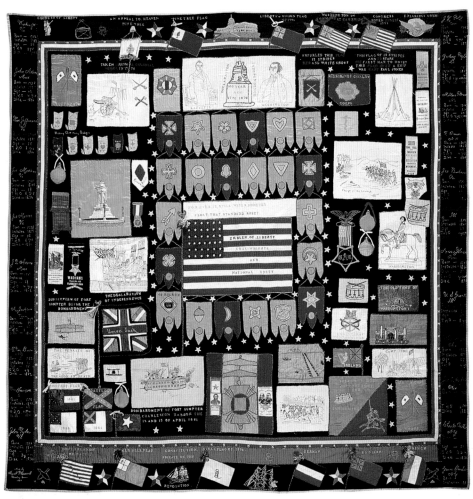

34. Appliqué and embroidered Crazy quilt, made by Mrs. N. W. Carswell, dated 1887, Waterbury, Connecticut. 70¾″ x 70½″. Various phrases come to mind such as "Sounding brass and tinkling cymbals," or "Hail to the Chief!" as one views this remarkably lavish example of a most lavish age. The eighteen men who had been elected president·by the time Mrs. Carswell made, signed, and dated her contribution to Victoriana are listed around the border in careful embroidery. Not only their names, but also their birth dates, dates of installation as president, age at the time, term of office, and death dates are recorded. Ships, foreign flags, battles, and as much historical trivia as possible are remembered in the center with embroidery, ribbons, and drawings. (Present whereabouts unknown)

35. Pieced cotton quilt of printed campaign kerchiefs, c. 1888. 79″ x 79″. The campaign of 1888 was won by the two gentlemen depicted in the elaborate blue kerchiefs, Benjamin Harrison and Levi P. Morton. If that "Tippecanoe and Morton too" line rings false to you, just remember the first, and more famous Harrison, William Henry (see figure 7) and his running mate, John Tyler. Benjamin was the grandson of the old general and found his war cry useful, especially as he was not himself a very popular or strong candidate. He ran what was known as a "front porch" campaign and won the presidency for the Republican Party, for one term only. Notice that some of the other vote-getting phrases on the kerchiefs with flags and eagles are "Protection" and "Home Industries," a recurrent theme in American politics. Photograph by Ken Burris. (The Shelburne Museum)

36. Pieced cotton quilt of scrap prints and printed commemorative kerchief, c. 1889. 83½" x 81". If the pair in the kerchief seem oddly matched, remember that Benjamin Harrison was famous for being the "Centennial President," one hundred years after the election of George Washington, so here they are together, from left to right, George Washington and Benjamin Harrison. The setting is a charming collection of scraps squares, representative of the wonderful cotton prints of the late nineteenth century. The Cleveland quilt (see figure 32) is so similar to this one that we can only wonder if the same maker was inspired by elections rather than parties: Cleveland, a Democrat, in 1884 and Harrison, a Republican, in 1888. (Collection of Great Expectations, Houston, Texas)

37. Pieced and appliqué dark blue polka-dot cotton on white cotton background, mid to late nineteenth century. 74" x 60". This style of eagle, with downturned wings, and striped shield, seems to appear more often after 1850. The small polka-dot fabric was also popular after the Civil War, but there are no other clues to the age or origin of these four handsome birds with their pieced border. (America Hurrah Antiques, N.Y.C.)

38. Pieced and reverse appliqué cotton quilt, Whig's Defeat, last quarter of the nineteenth century, northern Ohio. 82″ x 62″. Whig's Defeat is an intricate pattern that might also be called "Quilter's Defeat," except to a quilter as able as the one who made this beauty. The quilting in the open spaces is as spectacular as the piecing and delicate reverse appliqué on the five-leaf pieces at each corner of each block. Some of the quilting is worked in horn of plenty and fruit designs, with a background of cross-hatch lines. A true mark of the quilter's art is the almost perfect circle formed where any four of the pieced designs meet. See also figure 17 for another use of the Whig's Defeat block. (Collection of Joyce Aufderheide)

39. Pieced and appliqué cotton quilt, made by Mary Dunn LeRoy, c. 1898, Lakewood, New York. 70″ x 70″. Americans were not only on a patriotic spree during the Spanish-American War, but also they were totally enamored of the "heroes" of the Navy. Although Commodore George Dewey ("You can fire when ready, Gridley") seems to have outlasted his fellow Navy men, Richard P. Hobson and William T. Sampson, in the memory of most Americans, the latter two must have occupied a large place in the heart of this quiltmaker. Many of us probably recognize the phrase, "Remember the Maine," without an entirely clear idea of what the *Maine* was. It was, of course, the American ship that exploded and sank off the coast of Cuba on February 15, 1898, pushing the country ever closer to war with Spain. In recent years Admiral Hyman Rickover did some research that led to the conclusion that the ship had not been sabotaged, but had exploded from some internal problem. The historians, Morison and Commager, describing the mood of the country during the Spanish-American War, say: "It was more close and personal to Americans than World War I: it was their own little show for independence, fair play, and hip-hip-hurray democracy." (America Hurrah Antiques, N.Y.C.)

38

40. Pieced and appliqué cotton quilt, made by Mary Baxter, 1898, Kearny, New Jersey. 78″ x 76″. Was there ever a more delightful, more spirited, or more stunningly graphic example of a flag-waving American textile than this astonishing quilt? The Spanish-American War in 1898 brought forth a wild burst of patriotic enthusiasm, perhaps because it was the first war in which the North and South were once again united in common cause. The "hurrah" of flags on this masterly piece seems almost to be accompanying Teddy Roosevelt on his famous charge up San Juan Hill! Photograph courtesy America Hurrah Antiques, N.Y.C. (Museum of American Folk Art; gift of the Amicus Foundation, Anne Baxter Klee, and Trustees of the Museum of American Folk Art, 1985)

41. Pieced and appliqué solid-color and printed cottons on white cotton background, late nineteenth or early twentieth century, Connecticut. 97½″ x 94½″. The background is made of Nine Patch blocks alternating with solid white blocks, forming a sort of Single Irish Chain, sometimes called Kitty Corner. The border is of another Nine Patch, again alternating with solid white. These simple blocks in scrap fabrics and the very naïve eagle with his one arrow and spray of three leaves make us feel that this might well be a quilt made by a young girl learning her lessons in piecing and appliqué. It came from the Brown-Francis family homestead in Canterbury, Connecticut. (Smithsonian Institution)

42. Pieced and appliqué Royal Hawaiian quilt, *Ku'u Hae Aloha (My Beloved Flag)*, 1900–1910, Hawaiian Islands. 74″ x 74″. The flag established by the Hawaiian legislative council in 1845, and later adopted by the territorial government in 1925, bears some resemblance to the British flag with its combined crosses of St. Andrew, St. George, and St. Patrick. The eight red, white, and blue stripes represent the main islands in the Hawaiian group. Several of these pieces were made in a burst of island patriotism after the deposing of Queen Liliuokalani during the American-led revolution of 1893, and the lowering of the flag by the victors and new rulers of the islands. There is little resemblance between these strong red, white, and blue quilts and the more familiar Hawaiian quilt designs with flowing vines, leaves, and flowers, except the excellent echo quilting, a hallmark of all Hawaiian quilts. Photograph courtesy Thomas K. Woodard: American Antiques and Quilts, New York City. (Kiracofe and Kyle, San Francisco, California)

43. Pieced cotton premium flags from Sweet Caporal Cigarettes, c. 1917, Minnesota. 82″ x 70″. The fabric in these premium flags is rather like cotton flannel, not especially suitable to quilting. The backing is also an odd cloth of the late nineteenth and early twentieth centuries—flowered cretonne, an inferior home-decorating fabric. The quilt is finished with ties instead of quilting. The maker had a good sense of design, working the American flags and the flags of our possessions and protectorates of the time into a nice center panel. Around that panel are rows of American flags, then the flags of other nations, including some that no longer exist. A true World War I sense of revenge must have inspired the maker to put all the German flags down in reverse. (Collection of Joyce Aufderheide)

44. Pieced, appliqué, and embroidered cotton quilt, commemorating the Century of Progress Exhibition in Chicago, made by Mrs. W. B. Lathouse, 1933, Warren, Ohio. 82″ x 66″. From left to right the portraits are of highly recognizable heroes of American history, even though the large center one is unfinished. The inscription over this portrait of Franklin Delano Roosevelt (1933–1945) is "Hope of a Nation," making it possible that the lack of features is symbolic. Perhaps the maker of the quilt intended to fill them in after she was more sure of his performance in office. Washington is described as "Father of Our Country," and Lincoln as "The Emancipator." The square-rigger is the *Mayflower*, and the airship is the *Macon*. The many "modern conveniences" around the border make one sharply realize now that fifty years have passed and all things have changed. Note, for instance, the upright telephone, upright vacuum cleaner, and steam locomotive with coal car. Even the forty-eight stars on the flag date the piece, and certainly the bucolic farm scene can only be found in local museums! Photograph courtesy America Hurrah Antiques, N.Y.C. (Private collection)

45. Pieced, appliqué, and embroidered quilt, c. 1934. 84½″ x 73½″. The NRA blue eagle, together with the motto "We Do Our Part," is one of the most lasting symbols of Franklin D. Roosevelt's New Deal, in spite of the short life of the NRA itself, which was declared unconstitutional after only two years. The eagle, unlike his earlier cousins with their signs of war and peace, holds the cogwheel of industrial progress and bolts of lightning to symbolize the burgeoning electric power of America. Note the small embroidered dollar signs and the Prairie Point edges (little folds of cloth in red, white, and blue) on the quilt. The tassels made of grocery string are certainly appropriate, for every grocery store of the period displayed NRA posters or window stickers! (Franklin D. Roosevelt Library, Hyde Park, New York)

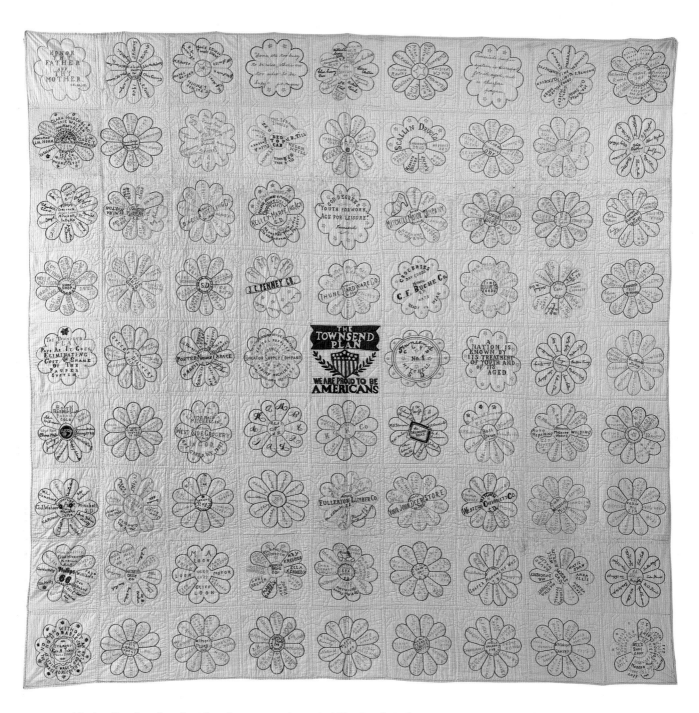

46. Appliqué and embroidered cotton quilt, mid-1930s, South Dakota. 96″ x 92″. For students of the Great Depression, this quilt should speak strongly. *The Townsend Plan* featured in the center block (along with *We Are Proud to Be Americans*) represented salvation to the many followers of Dr. Francis E. Townsend. It was the first attempt at an old-age plan, shortly before Social Security became a less generous reality. The basis of Townsend's plan was that each person over sixty should receive $200.00 a month, provided he would spend it in that same month, thereby pumping money into the almost stagnant economy. The fact that the federal government simply didn't have that kind of money did not seem to bother this dreamer or his supporters, many of whom were lucky if they made a standard wage of $50.00 to $100.00 a month. Many company names and lists of employees—most of them from towns in South Dakota—are included in the gaily embroidered blocks, several of which bear such inscriptions as "God decrees, 'Youth for work, age for leisure.'—Townsend." Not only was Dr. Townsend not successful—except in being one of the forces that pushed the government into a Social Security Act—but he was eventually investigated by Congress and cited for contempt, when he stalked out of the hearing. He tried his hand at unseating F.D.R. in a coalition with Gerald K. Smith and Father Coughlin under the Union Party banner in 1936, with predictable lack of success. (America Hurrah Antiques, N.Y.C.)

47. Pieced, appliqué, and embroidered quilt, *Historic U.S.A.*, 1936, Texas. 93″ x 75″. In the depths of the Great Depression, Fanny and Charles Normann, a husband-and-wife team, were commissioned by the late husband of Artie Fultz Davis of Navasota, Texas, to make this sesquicentennial piece. The signing of the Declaration of Independence is framed with portraits of the thirty-one presidents, with—perhaps significantly—Franklin Roosevelt's portrait just below that of George Washington. Flags, Liberty Bells, eagles, and the Statue of Liberty finish off this wonderfully patriotic piece with a flourish. (Courtesy of Mrs. Artie Fultz Davis and Star of the Republic Museum, Washington, Texas)

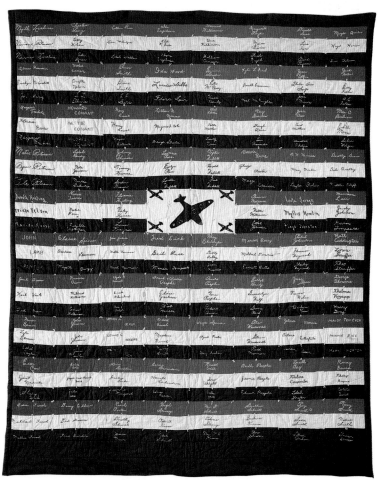

48. Pieced, appliqué, embroidered, and tied cotton quilt, made by the Rockford Bowling League of the Women's International Bowling Congress, 1940, Rockford, Michigan. 66″ x 78″. Raffle tickets and signatures were sold and the names were embroidered on this quilt—all to help the Women's International Bowling Congress raise money to buy the things that "our boys overseas" surely needed. Thousands of dollars were raised through many such small efforts and Congress presented the Army Air Force with a bomber for Christmas 1942, and another bomber in March 1943 was named Miss WIBC. There were also assorted ambulances and other hardware sent overseas by this patriotic group of women. A sidelight on this bit of patriotic history is the marriage of Marge Lang-West, who worked on the quilt, to Lawrence Price, who won it in the raffle. (Collection of Mr. and Mrs. Lawrence Price)

49. Pieced, appliqué, and embroidered cotton quilt, c. 1941, Texas. 93″ x 64″. The stolid little donkeys, symbol of the Democratic Party, leave no doubt about the political feelings of this quilter. She also was bold in her support of Roosevelt for a third term—embroidered straight across the center. The fabrics are typical of the 1930–1940 era. There were more of the bright pastel shades of solid-color cotton, like the melon shade of the background, at that time than ever before or since. A woman could easily make a dress of checked gingham for less than 50¢ and have enough left over to cut out the donkeys for her quilt. (Collection of Joyce Aufderheide)

50. Pieced, appliqué, and embroidered cotton quilt, made by Mrs. W. B. Lathouse, 1945, Warren, Ohio. 88″ x 76″. The patriotism of this professional seamstress and quilter, who came to America from Wales in 1922, could scarcely be in doubt (see also figure 44). Every possible symbol of the Allies of World War II has been worked into this marvelous red, white, and blue statement: Roosevelt, MacArthur, Stalin, Churchill, "the hands across the sea," Americans saluting the Stars and Stripes, and the flags of Britain (top), Russia (left), Australia (bottom), and China (right). Pansies are for remembrance (of Pearl Harbor), and the three dots and a dash, which are the letter V in Morse code, "V for Victory" signs. The Russian bear, American eagle, and British bulldog, all looking warlike, round out this posterlike quilt. Photograph courtesy America Hurrah Antiques, N.Y.C. (Private collection)

44

51. Pieced, appliqué, and embroidered cotton hanging, *Where Liberty Dwells*, made by Florence Peto, 1953, New Jersey. 53½″ x 44″. Florence Peto was a collector of and authority on quilts and American textiles. She combined these interests by making a number of small quilts or hangings with the antique fabrics she collected. This one is so full of patriotic symbols—eagles, Liberty, George Washington, the Liberty Bell, and even the cherries of that myth about the young George Washington—that it would take a long time to identify them all. The Medallion arrangement is her own, symbolic of the early American quilts so often in this style. (Peto Collection)

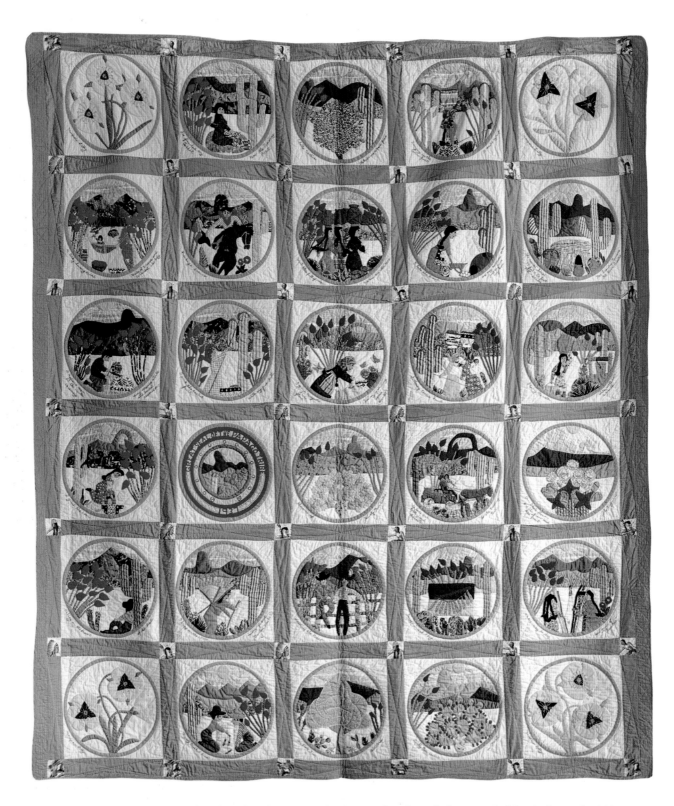

52. Pieced, appliqué, and embroidered cotton quilt, designed and made by Mrs. Goldie Richmond, 1966, Papago Reservation, Arizona. 91½″ x 81½″. This amazing work of folk art is one of seven made by Mrs. Goldie Richmond, wife of a trader who lived on the Papago Reservation. She was known as the "Angel of the Papagos," and it is obvious that she took great interest in the people and their daily lives. She worked directly in the fabric without preliminary drawings to create intricate scenes from reservation life. Some blocks depict desert scenes, cowboys, children at play, and bread making. Third row up, second from the left is the great seal of the Papagos. In each corner is a bunch of the beautiful mariposa lilies that grow on the reservation. The sashing is arranged to make long-pointed stars between the blocks, and the small corner blocks are cut from a cotton print of the time, depicting Indians in various poses and headdress. Photograph by Myron Miller. (Arizona State Museum, Tucson, Arizona)

53. Pieced and embroidered cotton quilt, made by George Russell's fourth grade in the Prince Street School, 1976, New Haven, Connecticut. 86″ x 56″. Not only did grown women and quilt groups come to life in the Bicentennial period to create memorials to this country's 200 years, but also grade-school children learned sewing and history as they quilted their own records of the time. These twenty-one children of ages nine to twelve chose their fabric, researched quilt patterns to find this one called Monkey Wrench, sewed the blocks, and embroidered their names around the border—all under the supervision of a male teacher. They used red, white, and blue and finished the corners with the Bicentennial symbol. They were justly proud of the results and presented the quilt to President and Mrs. Gerald Ford with a letter that said in part, "We simply couldn't think of persons more important than you to receive this product of our effort." (Gerald R. Ford Museum, Grand Rapids, Michigan)

54. Pieced quilt, designed and made by Alice Hegy and Arnold Savage, 1876–1976, Ohio. 81″ x 81″. Not many quilts span several generations in the making, as is the case here. The enthusiasm of some Centennial quilters probably soon faded, and their efforts were consigned to a century of dark trunks and musty attics. At least that is what happened to the burst of patriotism that made Alice Hegy start this vibrant red-white-and-blue gem at the time of the Centennial celebration in 1876. Fortunately, her talented great-nephew, Arnold Savage, discovered the center section in time to add the border of sawtooth strips and flags for the 1976 Bicentennial. The flags are, of course, those of the United States and Ohio, home of both quilters. Photograph by Myron Miller. (Collection of the artist)

55. Appliqué and embroidered *Putnam Valley Quilt*, designed by Gladys Boalt, © 1976, Putnam Valley, New York. 108″ x 86″. Nineteen women, who at the beginning could not have realized the magnitude of the undertaking, decided to make a "truly different" Bicentennial quilt with real historical significance. The research, alone, might have stopped many people, but the enthusiasm of the designer, Gladys Boalt, carried them through. She attributes their success to the fact "that it is the nature of women to work well together most of the time." What resulted is a complete history lesson about Putnam County at the time of the Revolution, when it was, in fact, still a part of Dutchess County. It was named in 1814 for General Israel Putnam, who is portrayed at top right on his horse. Many ordinary citizens, going about their daily life in home, school, and church, can also be seen in great detail on this exquisite Bicentennial quilt. (Private collection)

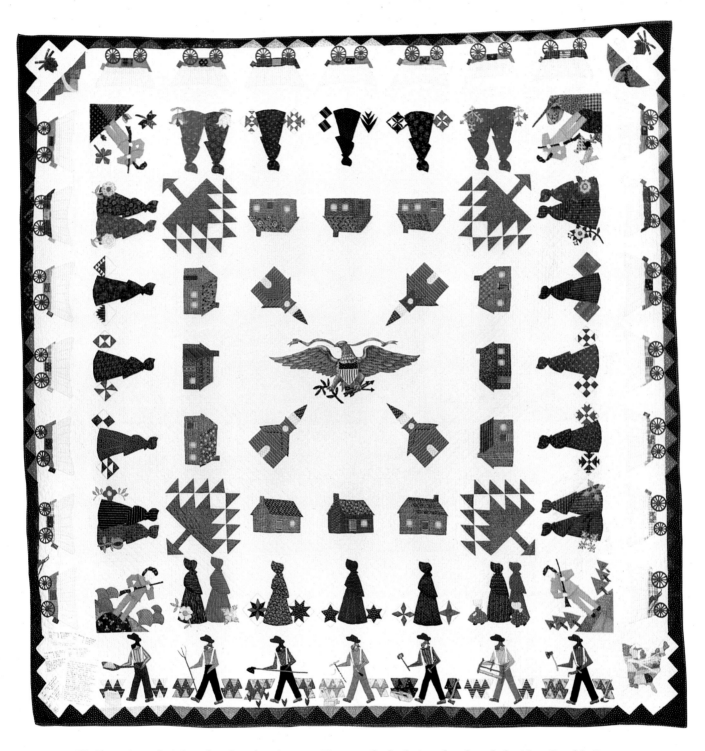

56. Pieced, appliqué, and embroidered cotton *Heritage Quilt*, designed and made by Mary Pemble Barton, and quilted by women of St. Petri Lutheran Church, 1976, Ames, and Story City, Iowa. 101″ x 102″. Fabrics as much as a hundred years old, and fabrics of the Bicentennial period were all worked together in this recollection of the historic migration to Iowa of both Mary Pemble Barton's ancestors and the many others who trekked those long miles. The women, each with her own quilt block, and the men with their building and farming tools, march serenely, moving ever westward. The eagle in the center is reminiscent of the eagle in the quilts of the 1840s, when Iowa was settled. It took Mary Pemble Barton nearly eight years to bring her *Heritage Quilt* to completion. Photograph by Rae Gene Studios. (Collection of the artist)

57. Pieced and appliqué quilt top, *Of Thee I Sing*, designed and made by Jean Mitchell, © 1977, Lawrence, Kansas. 90″ x 90″. Begun in 1976 as a Bicentennial project, this quilt top reached completion a year later but was not quilted. The Medallion style is an echo of quilts of the late eighteenth and early nineteenth centuries. The Pine Tree is a very early American quilt pattern, as are many of the stars. The style of the leaves, vines, and birds is much like crewel embroidery of late Colonial days. The eagle sits atop the Pine Tree with thirteen stars around him representing the original Colonies. Under the tree Martha Washington, in front of Mount Vernon, waves farewell to George Washington, astride his horse. The large flowers in the four corner baskets represent the first settlers: carnation for Spain, rose for England, iris for France, and tulip for Holland, Sweden, and Germany. Each appliqué is outlined with chain stitch to give the delicate figures a strong definition. (Collection of the artist)

58. Pieced cotton quilt, Burgoyne Surrounded, made by the Yankee Pride Quilters, 1984–1985, Vermont. 106″ x 89″. In 1777 at Saratoga, New York, the previously successful British general, "Gentleman Johnny" Burgoyne, along with six thousand of his troops, was surrounded and captured by General Horatio Gates. The stark outlines of this quilt pattern are said to represent the battle plan of that memorable day. The design is usually worked in dark on light fabrics, but the seven women of the Yankee Pride group in Burlington, Vermont, chose a more startling combination. They have a plan by which each member will receive one of their beautiful group-made quilts, in order of age. Louise Ripley. the second member to acquire a quilt, and now the proud owner of this one, says that she is willing to redecorate her entire bedroom to accommodate it. The traditional values of a group of women quilting for each other, and the historical significance of the design seem closely bound. (Collection of Louise Ripley)

59. Pieced, appliqué, and embroidered cotton quilt, assembled by the Boise Peace Quilt Project, 1984, Boise, Idaho. 108″ x 132″. The drawings, one from each of the fifty states, were done by children and translated into needlework by the women of the Boise Project. This quilt is being sent to every senator who signs up to sleep one night under it—and to tell about his dreams of peace. The unusual group, dedicated to world peace, began their quilting with a friendship quilt for Russia. When it was finished, four of the women traveled to Washington, D.C., in May 1982, to present it at the Russian Embassy, where it was accepted by the cultural affairs attachés and passed on to the Soviet Women's Committee. There have been at least twelve other "Peace Project" quilts made in the time between these two, and many more are to come in future years. Photograph by Michael Cordell. (Boise Peace Quilt Project)

EXPRESSIONS
OF
LIBERTY

Statue of Liberty by Helen Cargo, Tuscaloosa, Alabama. 1985–1986. 70″ x 72″. Cotton, linen, and polyesters. The artist feels very strongly about the ideals represented by the Statue of Liberty. She included immigrants from many countries in the borders of her Center Medallion quilt. In order to obtain an increased sense of realism, rough linen was used for the raft, and a small number of synthetic fabrics appear in other areas. In the seventeenth, eighteenth, and nineteenth centuries quilting techniques were often handed from one generation to another within a family. This quilt is dedicated to the maker's mother. An inscription on the reverse side reads: *To my mother who taught me how to sew and quilt and to care about the tired, the poor, and the homeless.* Helen Cargo's grandmother, her great-grandmother, and her great, great-grandmother were also accomplished quilters. Although the artist has been quilting for over fifteen years, this is the first contest she has entered. Her husband collects antique quilts and owns an impressive group of nineteenth- and early twentieth-century examples. Many quilters are introduced to the craft by collecting.

Centennial by Judy Hopkins, Anchorage, Alaska. 1985. 72″ x 71½″. Cotton. Many needle artists have great difficulty finding a title that pleases them after thay have completed their quilt. The process can become a family affair. "My vocal, opinionated family members blackballed my preferred title: *Starship Liberty*. These same people have always assigned appropriate weight to my creative activities, giving me lots of time and room, so are allowed their opinions." The design for *Centennial* evolved slowly over a four-month period. Conceived as a rectangle, it seemed impossible to make the design fit a square, so the artist decided to utilize triangles to create her visual image. Execution of the quilt took more than 400 hours that extended over three months. Judy Hopkins has been quilting for nearly five years and has created several quilts that have won local and national recognition. She is a member of the Anchorage Log Cabin Quilters and has a particular fondness for her craft. It is very much a family activity: "My husband frequently reads to me while I quilt—a real bonus."

From Nine Patch to the Future by Marla M. Hattabaugh, Scottsdale, Arizona. 1985–1986. 72″ x 72″. Cotton and some cotton blends. During the early days of quilting in America few could afford the luxury of purchasing fabrics to stitch a quilt. As old clothing wore out, the sturdy parts were washed and saved to be used again for making a bedcover or a rug. Many of the fabrics in this example are old and were given to the maker by friends who gather weekly at the First United Methodist Church of Scottsdale, where they attend a modern form of the traditional quilting bee. The artist frequently uses old cloth and refers to herself as a scrap quilter or a salvage artist. A small black-and-white Nine Patch created from old fabrics is a traditional design used in eighteenth- and nineteenth-century quilts. In this quilt it is a symbol of the past. The light from the Statue of Liberty's torch forms the quilting design that extends over the entire central portion. Marla Hattabaugh believes this is one of her most successful quilts. "It was the first time that I felt like a real artist. It was so natural. Everything went together very nicely. I learned a lot about quilting from this piece. My quilts in the future will all be different."

Immigrant's Hope by Judy Tipton, Little Rock, Arkansas. 1985. 72″ x 72″. Cotton and cotton blends. Television influences contemporary life in many ways. The artist that made this quilt was inspired by the television movie *Ellis Island* and was especially touched by the immigrants viewing the Statue of Liberty for the first time. "Thoughts and emotions of leaving a homeland for a new and unknown future must have been mixed and varied. This is the feeling I have tried to capture in the faces on the quilt." Originally, an appliqué design of a sheaf of wheat ran around the outside and inside borders. "After hours of appliqué and embroidery, I displayed it to my husband. He asked, 'Why the waterbugs?' By no stretch of the imagination did my wheat look like wheat! Out came the ripper and back to the drawing board." Judy Tipton has been quilting for three years and is a member of the Arkansas Quilters Guild, Inc. Her first quilt won first place at the 1985 Arts, Crafts and Design Fair. She began this quilt on July 4th and completed it on December 20, 1985, logging nearly 1,200 hours for her project.

Freedom Wreath by A. Diann Logan, Denver, Colorado. 1985–1986. 71¾″ x 72.″ Cotton. Freedom is a favorite theme for the artist who has used the idea in several of the eighty-nine quilts she has completed since 1975. This quilt, her first appliqué piece, has deep personal meaning to its maker. "When I look at this quilt, I always think of my best friend of eleven years—Borfus—my big black furry dog who died July 1st. Other dog lovers will understand when I say my grief nearly got the best of me. This quilt gave structure to my days, drove me crazy, but kept me sane. Many tears fell on this piece but I kept stitching." Diann Logan worked approximately 2,600 hours designing and making this quilt. "I worked on the quota system. The quilt was designed and cut out during May and construction began on June 1st. I gave myself two months to do the center medallion and three weeks for each border. I then divided the number of pieces to be appliquéd by the number of days allotted and had my daily quota: thirteen pieces per day in the center, seventeen pieces a day in the borders. Quilting began October 28, 1985, and the quilt was completed January 12, 1986. The average working day was from 6 A.M. to 10 A.M., and if I got ahead in my quota, I got a day off. My calendar says I had six days off during that time, but I don't remember them. This quilt consumed my life." The artist has won several prizes for her quilts and thirteen of her original quilt designs have been published in magazines. She is the author of *Designs in Patchwork*, which will be released by Oxmoor House in 1987.

Of Thee I Sing by Pat Karambay, Newington, Connecticut. 1985–1986. 72″ x 72″. 100% cotton. Red-and-white Schoolhouse quilts were very popular during the nineteenth century. The motif is especially appropriate for this artist because she was once an elementary school teacher. Her fondness for patriotic music is reflected through the inclusion of song titles that enclose the schoolhouses. Most quilters discover special pleasures in their work. "When I was making this piece, it was the first time in a long time that I had thought in depth about my own pride in being an American. One of the wonderful things about quilting is that there are times in the process when your mind is free and your hands continue to do the mechanical parts unconsciously. I believe a quilt must be functional. It is something that must warm people physically and mentally. A quilt must also have an interesting visual design and be made with lots of love and feeling. I've only been making quilts for two years. My first effort won Best First Quilt at the prestigious Northfield Quilt Festival in Vermont in 1985. I'm hooked! I'll go on." Pat Karambay felt certain her quilt would win national recognition, for two occurrences in her life uncannily related to her project. While waiting for a bus, she casually read her horoscope, which advised "...you have an audience waiting which is friendly and wants you to be a winner." On another occasion, when leaving a fabric shop, she happened to kick an empty snuff tin that had a portrait of the Statue of Liberty on its cover.

Dear Lady by Iran Lawrence, Newark, Delaware. 1985. 70″ x 70″. Cotton and Dacron. This meticulously conceived quilt bursts with symbolism and imagery. The artist chose the popular Center Medallion design which she enriched with a Liberty torch and an eagle's wings that represent pride and strength. The torch stands for freedom and the bell for liberty. The thirteen blue stars above the eagle refer to the thirteen original Colonies. The gold arrows under the eagle's wings symbolize the several wars America has fought to preserve peace and liberty in the world. White stars—one for each state—float on a dark-blue background. Iran Lawrence is a professional artist and a well-known custom quilt designer. She is a member of the American Craft Council, is a fine-arts photographer, and holds a B.S. in Economics. She has been quilting for approximately four years.

America in Appliqué by Marilyn Dorwart, Delray Beach, Florida. 1985–1986. 72″ x 71¾″. Cotton and cotton blends. Many contemporary quilters prefer the appliqué technique to piecing, for it allows them to create more freely. Like the maker of this quilt, many consider working with appliqué as "painting in fabric." The design of this piece records some of America's most important moments, and some of the motifs were inspired by well-known folk paintings from the eighteenth and nineteenth centuries. An American eagle flanked by draped flags centers the top and provides a formal patriotic touch as well. Marilyn Dorwart is from a family with a strong quilting tradition over several generations. She works with "... markings from the mid-1800s to the present day used by my grandmother and my great- and great-great-grandmothers as they made quilts." In addition to quilting the artist works in several other craft areas. Among her favorites are flower arranging, making soft sculpture, and doing calligraphy. She began quilting in 1976 and is a member of the Gold Coast Quilters Guild, the Delray Quilt Guild, and the Southern Handcraft Society. She worked nearly nine months to create this quilt.

Of Thee I Sing by Barbara Thurman Butler, Marietta, Georgia. 1985–1986. 72″ x 72″. Cotton and cotton blends. The design of this quilt shows the head and right arm of the Statue of Liberty silhouetted against the American flag, New York City, New York Harbor, and surrounded by immigrants. Fireworks have been quilted in the flag. "These seemed a natural symbol of the joy of freedom the immigrants who must have felt when they first saw the Statue . . ." The artist has embroidered the flag with the names of the people who inspired, originated the idea, designed, built, supported, or raised funds for the Statue of Liberty. Also embroidered are the names of immigrants who contributed to the building of the nation and the evolution of American life. The embroidered initials on the white stars stand for the U.S. presidents who significantly helped to pass immigration laws or assisted with the preservation of the Statue. Barbara Butler has also been involved with the restoration of the Statue. "After watching me work on my quilt, my two-year-old daughter decided to 'help' while I was out of the room. She stuck a lot of pins in it then cut eight holes trying to 'copy Mama.' So I say my Statue of Liberty has been under reconstruction too. She and my son also 'named' four of the immigrants: 'Morgan, Blake and Mom and Dad—our family.' " The artist began teaching herself to quilt in 1975 and in 1982 took her first formal class. She is a member of East Cobb Quilters Guild and spent about 300 hours finishing this piece.

Liberty Quilt by Helen Mary Friend, Honolulu, Hawaii. 1985. 71¾″ x 71½″. Cotton, cotton-polyester mix, nylon polyester, and transparent organza. Most of the individual blocks used to form the central section of this quilt were fashioned in patterns that were popular in the eighteenth and nineteenth centuries. Many of today's quilt-makers combine design motifs from the past with creative ideas of their own, producing textiles that are unique to our time. The quiltmaker is an immigrant herself. As a child of five in England she began her first needlework efforts and focused upon the sewing of clothes and the execution of embroidery. She was introduced to quilting in Hawaii when she enrolled as a student of the well-known teacher Pam Jaasko. This is the only quilt completed by Helen Friend. She is a member of the Hawaii Stitchery and Fiber Arts Guild and attends most of the monthly meetings. This educational group is open to all ethnic groups and to all ages.

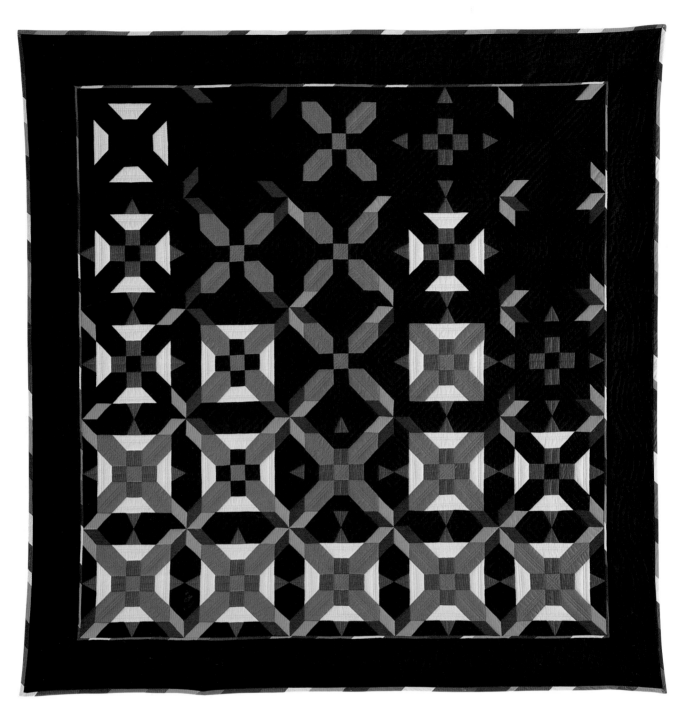

The Melting Pot: Our Heritage by Joyce Stewart, Rexburg, Idaho. 1985–1986. 73″ x 73″. Cottons. The symbolism developed by the maker of this quilt is complex but beautiful. "The Statue of Liberty is a symbol of freedom to all those who were here, to those who have come here, and to those who wish to come here to make America their home. America has become known as the melting pot because our nation's heritage is made up of people from almost every country on the face of the earth. In my quilt I have tried to represent this. In the top row of blocks each block has just one color. Each of these colors represents an individual or a nation. In the next row of blocks I have added one more color to each block signifying that we are starting to come together as a whole. This process is repeated until we reach the bottom row where all the blocks are exactly alike—indicating that these individuals from different countries have been transformed into a melting pot of people, traditions, and ideas. I have tried to make my quilt a symbol of all the things which the Statue of Liberty stands for: our heritage, our freedom, our strength and unity, our brotherly love and binding together to become one. To the Statue of Liberty: May your torch burn forever bright!" Joyce Stewart is a member of the Utah Quilt Guild and has won many first prizes including a Best of Show for her imaginative creations. She spent 250–300 hours making this quilt.

Freedom's Children by Sidney Allee Miller, Galena, Illinois. 1986. 72″ x 72″. Cotton. A crowd gathers at the base of the Statue of Liberty to celebrate, and her shadow falls across them. The descendants of immigrants, free to gather, come in their diversity to honor this symbol of liberty. The appliquéd abstract forms, the featureless faces, the myriad colors present "the melting pot" that is America. Fifty stars have been quilted into the fabric to represent the states. The artist received great encouragement and support from her family. "The idea was an exciting one and my family wanted me to do it. They said they would put up with the mess for seven months and do whatever was necessary to leave me free to put in an average of three hours a night to finish it. I work full time as an advertising designer for a publishing company." Sidney Miller spent about 600 hours creating this piece. Although she belongs to no formal quilt guilds, she lectures on the ". . . evolution of quilt patterns and quilts as America's only folk art." She had entered a competition only once before, and her piece won a blue ribbon.

Liberty is the one thing you can't have unless you give it to others.
W.A.White
Those who expect to reap the blessings of freedom must undergo the fatigue of sup-porting it.
T.Paine
Ask not what your country can do for you, but what you can do for your country.
J.F. Kennedy
Give me your huddled masses yearn-ing to breathe free... I lift my lamp beside the golden door.
Emma Lazarus
26

Surrounding Liberty by Mary Kay Horn, Indianapolis, Indiana. 1986. 70″ x 74″. Cottons, cotton blends, Ultrasuede, and corduroy. The artist who crafted this textile especially enjoys making quilts for contests. She finds it fun to read the rules and attempt to develop a design that will win. While working at a clerical job, the idea for this piece came to her. She used her break to sketch the figures on adding-machine tape. The figures in the inner border represent all Americans and include immigrants from different time periods, numerous countries, and several occupations. Mary Kay Horn believes this quilt is "...the most fun thing I ever did. I so much enjoyed the comments of everyone who saw it while I was working on it." Her husband is most supportive of her quilting efforts. "He says I have turned him into a wealthy man. Who but a wealthy man can sleep under a $500 blanket?" The artist has taught quilting in the Indianapolis public school system and is a member of the Quilt Guild of Indianapolis and a workshop group, I Q's. In this needlework group, which has frequent meetings that are like a twentieth-century quilting bee, she feels she has "...gained the sisters I never had."

The Lady Liberty Medallion Quilt by Marianne Fons, Winterset, Iowa. 1986. 72″ x 72″. Cotton. The artist had very specific ideas about the design of this quilt. "The theme of 'Liberty, Freedom and the Heritage of America in honor of the Statue of Liberty Centennial' is executed in my quilt by symbolic patchwork and appliqué motifs. The face of Liberty is framed first by large triangular areas containing Ocean Waves patchwork, representing the oceans crossed for more than four centuries by Pilgrims, Colonists, settlers, immigrants, and refugees to the free world, as well as Liberty's position in New York Harbor. The middle border is composed of traditional American patchwork quilt blocks whose names, I feel, relate to liberty, America's heritage, and the Statue itself. The blocks are named (beginning at the top center and moving clockwise): All Kinds, Hopes and Wishes, French Star, Brave New World, and Prosperity Block. The outer border is a continuous vine of American Beauty roses and buds, symbolizing the growth and beauty of American culture, as well as the growth of our country's families. At each corner of the outer border is a pair of blue trumpet flowers, heralding the 100th birthday of the Lady Liberty, the world's greatest symbol of freedom." Marianne Fons has been quilting for nine years. She spent about 200 hours making the top of the quilt and 150 hours quilting it. She is a member of the Heritage Quilters of Winterset, Iowa, Quilters Guild, and the American International Quilt Association.

Oh, Beautiful by Suzanne Warren Brown, Arkansas City, Kansas. 1985. 72" x 72". Cotton, cotton blends, and polished cotton. While returning home from a fabric-buying trip with friends the artist discussed The Great American Quilt Contest. They began to sing all the patriotic songs they could remember and the idea for a panoramic view of the United States with the Statue of Liberty overlooking the country came to her. When they sang "America the Beautiful," she knew she wanted the Statue draped in the flag. The border of the finished quilt was also suggested by the song and is called "from sea to shining sea." Embroidery has been used to enhance the stars on the flag. The quilting in the blue area surrounding the map of the USA is a continuation of the sea-border motif and is intended to remind the viewer that the Statue came to America from across the sea. The fields across the map have been contour quilted to create depth. Added dimension has also been given to the trees and the Statue's face by touches of embroidery. Suzanne Warren Brown has been quilting for ten years and worked from August 1, 1985, to December 20, 1985, to make this piece. She is a member of the Walnut Valley Quilt Guild, Prairie Quilt Guild, and the Kaw Valley Quilt Guild. She has won many prizes for her quilting efforts and has won Best in Show awards in both local and national competitions.

Mother of Exiles by Rebekka Seigel, Owenton, Kentucky. 1985–1986. 72″ x 72″. Cotton and polyester blends. When the artist first began to consider her imagery for this quilt, she planned to show several immigrants in their native costumes in poses similar to that of the Statue of Liberty. This did not work out so she focused on "women who had something to do with freedom for other people here in America." She finally chose to represent the Pilgrim Anne Hutchinson who believed that women had the right to hold positions of authority in the church; Betsy Ross, who stitched the first American flag; Harriet Tubman, who led slaves to freedom in the North; Susan B. Anthony, who struggled to obtain voting rights for women; Emma Lazarus, who worked tirelessly to bring the Statue of Liberty to the United States; and Eleanor Roosevelt, who worked so hard in the area of human rights. The artist has been making quilts for over ten years. She is married to a potter and she and her husband are planning their first exhibit together. The quilt was made in a remarkably short period of time—one month! Rebekka Seigel teaches quiltmaking and specializes in the area of pictorial appliqué. She encourages her students to create their own designs and not rely upon quilting patterns from the past.

Miss Liberty by Deborah Sims, Kenner, Louisiana. 1985–1986. 71½" x 72". Cotton and cotton blends. Traditional Log Cabin blocks in the Courthouse Steps design were used to create this striking quilt. The Log Cabin blocks represent the "pioneer spirit of America," and the stars quilted in the border represent the USA today. Log Cabin quilts first became popular in the 1860s. Many different designs were developed from the various combinations of narrow rectangles and small squares of fabric. Few examples have an inner lining, and consequently they are seldom quilted. Ornate quilting usually appears only on open borders. Most Log Cabin quilts are "tufted" or tied to the backing. The artist chose to quilt this piece because "The Statue of Liberty represents freedom to all Americans and to people from visiting nations." The artist is a first-grade teacher. When her pupils learned that she was making a quilt for The Great American Quilt Contest, they insisted on knowing about her progress. At the time of the Mardi Gras they held a small parade and created a float with the Statue of Liberty on it to honor their teacher. Deborah Sims has been quilting for over three years. She has never entered a contest nor has she exhibited her pieces in exhibitions. It took nearly seven months to conceive, design, and finish this piece.

American Bison Spirit Heritage Quilt by Hilary A. Ervin, Waterville, Maine. 1985. 72″ x 72½″, excluding fringe.
Cotton blends and natural-color sheep's-wool yarn. Since much of this quilt is hand painted, colorfast procion
dyes were also used. A stylized eagle with wings made of American flags is surrounded by rows of bison and
their spirit shadows that "...stand for the millions of these animals slain in the second half of the nineteenth
century. The little blue eagles are a strength symbol bridging American Indian lore and America's official bird,
the eagle." The red, white, and blue bunting at the left and right sides are stylized flags, and the borders at the
top and bottom represent Indian contributions to America's arts. This quilt was inspired by the artist's concern
for animals. "All of my precious quilted works are coats with endangered animal themes—pandas, white tigers,
etc. The buffalo and the American eagle were chosen to represent America. Most appropriate for a heritage
theme American quilt." Hilary Ervin is an artist in many areas. She is an accomplished embroiderer, a dress-
maker, a fine artist, and a photographer. She has been quilting for five years and is a member of In Stitches.

Miss Liberty by Yvonne M. Khin, Bethesda, Maryland. 1985. 71½″ x 72¼″. Cotton and cotton blends. The artist immigrated to America from Burma in the 1940s. As she passed the Statue of Liberty at dawn, the great symbol of America exerted a profound influence on her. She still recalls the excitement of becoming part of a nation of nations—a country where all enjoy the opportunity of liberty and freedom. Traditional quilting patterns have been used to form the blocks in the outside border. Each block has been embroidered with the name of a state capital. The sixty-nine human figures in the foreground indicate the rich diversity of the American people. They also illustrate a special interest of the maker, who especially enjoys doing appliqué. The white background behind the figure of Liberty is quilted with a representation of the New York skyline and the Brooklyn Bridge. Yvonne Khin has been quilting for seventeen years. She first became interested in needlework in her native Burma, where sewing is part of the school curriculum. She does not belong to quilting guilds or professional organizations, for she feels too much emphasis is placed on social events and not enough attention is paid to quilting.

Light of Liberty by Carol Anne Grotrian, Quincy, Massachusetts. 1985–1986. 72″ x 72″. Cottons and hand-dyed fabric. Previous experience with hand-dyed fabrics made it possible for the artist to make the light radiating from Liberty's torch the central symbol of this quilt. The bird's-eye view of the Statue of Liberty and Bedloe's Island on which she stands is fascinatingly original and startlingly powerful. The artist recalled: "The deadline made quilting over Christmas a necessity, even on the plane home. With the chaos of excited children and adults, never-ending Christmas cookies and eggnog, near misses were a continual threat. The biggest problem came at the end of quilting. I mark as I go, made a mistake, and the last corner came out wrong. This required removing stitches and remaking a sizable portion. One large patch was damaged in the process. I held my breath and appliquéd a new piece on top. It's not detectable, but I learned how fragile and resilient quilts can be." Carol Anne Grotrian currently works as an office manager in an architectural firm. She has taught art, art history, and held numerous positions at universities across the country. She has long been interested in the crafts and began quilting in 1979, although her first full-size quilt for a bed was not started until 1982. She is a member of the New England Quilters Guild and has won several prizes and awards for quilts, including Best in Show.

History 101 by Isolde Sarnecki-de Vries, Ypsilanti, Michigan. 1985–1986. 72″ x 72″. Cotton and cotton blends. The Mariner's Compass that highlights the center of this quilt (with the eagle of the Great Seal created in stuffed work below) was chosen by the artist to indicate that immigrants had come to America from all parts of the world. The diamond that frames the compass has triangular segments in the pattern called Trip Around the World, symbolizing the great distance many of the immigrants traveled to seek their new life in America. The artist divided her appliqué "pictorial history" into two parts. One part illustrates scenes from the lives of the native Americans of the plains and Southwest; the other part is devoted to images evoking the immigrants from other lands. A quilt is a fragile work: the artist's children managed to stain her piece with chocolate and peanut butter. "I attempted to get it out with a stain remover which is *not* the thing to do. It bleached. I had to repair the quilt after it was quilted. You can tell in the Statue in the lower right corner. Also, I copied the Statue from a history-book cover that was printed from a reversed negative. I did not realize this until mid-December when I had a fourth of the appliqué still to do. Hence I had no time to take it out, and you will see the Statue with the wrong arm raised. For a quilt in honor of the Statue of Liberty, it was the Statue that kept me grinding my teeth." Isolde Sarnecki-de Vries has been quilting only since 1984. She dedicated this piece to her father-in-law, who recently passed away, for he provided her with some of the information that she used while designing her quilt.

Freedom to Dream by Carol Wagner, Roseville, Minnesota. 1985–1986. 72″ x 72″. Cotton and cotton blends. The unusual pose of the Statue of Liberty in this quilt reflects the artist's deep respect for the durability of the Statue both as symbol of the United States and as a sculptural object of immense importance. The names of many of the most famous women in history are quilted in the white background. "The women represented in my quilting stitches personify the opportunities for the freedom and liberty offered by our American heritage. While the Statue of Liberty convalesces from her repairs, she can rest and contemplate the achievements and endurance of American women. She's seated because this has been her time to rest and be reflective." Carol Wagner has been quilting for about ten years, but has spent considerably more time on her work in the last five or six years. She is a member of the Minnesota Quilters, Inc., and several satellite groups of Minnesota Quilters, such as Diverse Directions. She spent nearly a month planning this quilt before designing and making it, which took about 425 hours. She has had several of her quilted wall hangings published by Oxmoor House.

An American Portrait by Sally Smith, Columbus, Mississippi. 1986. 72″ x 71¾″. Cotton and cotton blends. The artist chose a three-quarter-length view of the Statue of Liberty as her central panel for this quilt. She has surrounded it with portraits of six immigrants and has embroidered a stanza from the famous poem "The New Colossus" by Emma Lazarus. The design was partially inspired by photographs from *A Nation of Immigrants* by John Kennedy. "Yes, I studied letters written by immigrants about their new homeland and about the hardships they encountered trying to get to America; and while embroidering the eyes of the elderly woman, I thought about what she must have gone through and it made me cry." Sally Smith has been quilting for four years and is a member of the Golden Triangle Quilters Guild. She spent over 625 hours designing and making this quilt. When asked what she would do with the $20,000 Grand Prize if she won The Great American Quilt Contest, she replied, "I've promised the Lord the first 10% and of course the IRS would get their share; after that we would want to put it toward the buying of a home as we now rent."

Lady Liberty by Lea Hillis, Lee's Summit, Missouri. 1985–1986. 71½″ x 71″. Cotton and cotton blends. The Statue of Liberty proudly stands in front of a map of the United States emblazoned with the Stars and Stripes. The design was inspired by a speech written about the Statue of Liberty by the artist when she was in the sixth grade, and "I've had a soft spot in my heart for her ever since." The artist submitted her work to The Great American Quilt Contest in a photo finish. "I completed the quilt on Sunday afternoon before the entry deadline and had my father take pictures. My sister picked the slides up from the developer on Wednesday. They were absolutely black! Dad's flash was not synchronized with the shutter. My sister called me at work and told me and I cried. She remained calm and went to the store for another roll of film. I ran home, got the quilt and with the help of two neighbor ladies took another roll of pictures and found an overnight slide-processing lab in Kansas City. At home, after work, I explained the day's events to my husband. He examined the camera to discover an incorrect setting, which meant the second roll of slides would be grossly overexposed. I cried again. He remained calm and went for another roll of film—48 hours to deadline. He set up lights and camera to photograph the quilt and checked all settings twice. I contacted a photographer friend who sent our slides to his lab with a 200% rush order. The slides were picked up at 3:00 P.M. on Thursday and sent by Express Mail to arrive on Friday by 5:00 P.M. Yeah! I made it!—with a lot of help from my friends!" The artist has been quilting for over ten years.

In God, Liberty, and Freedom We Trust by Shirley Barrett, Kalispell, Montana. 1985–1986. 72″ x 72″. Cotton and cotton blends. The head of the Statue of Liberty has been made the center of the handsome eight-rayed star, while four shield-body eagles embroidered in turkey red adorn the four corners. Two Liberty Bells, a picture of George Washington, and an American flag are also embroidered on the quilt. The artist has been quilting for five years and is a member of the Flathead Quilt Guild and the Quilters Art Guild of the Rocky Mountains. She has won several blue ribbon and two Best in Show prizes for her pieces in national and local quilt competitions. She worked about three months on this piece, which she took great care in designing. This is "the first quilt I've made where I had to use the encyclopedia and check out books from the library, only to discover that the best picture of 'the Lady' was right on my husband's baseball cap."

The Promise by Paulette Peters, Elkhorn, Nebraska. 1985. 72″ x 72″. Cotton and cotton blends. This pictorial quilt was inspired by a book of photographs of Ellis Island. The artist has consciously used perspective to suggest movement toward the land that promises liberty and freedom. Plain fabrics were used in the landscape to symbolize the relative freshness of America: "...an unwritten story in contrast to the darker, more elaborately decorated prints in the border, which are meant to imply the 'storied pomp of ancient lands' that the newcomers are leaving behind. The silhouetted figures represent humanity...people of any age, from any era in the last 100 years, wearing the costume of any country." Paulette Peters has been quilting for ten years. She is a member of the Cottonwood Quilters, Omaha Quilters Guild, Linclon Quilters Guild, and the Nebraska State Quilt Guild. Her quilts have been awarded prizes at several quilt shows and festivals. She spent over 100 hours executing this piece.

Liberty by Julia S. French, Las Vegas, Nevada. 1985–1986. 72″ x 72″. Cotton and cotton blends. Inspiration for a quilt design can come from many different sources: words from a favorite song, a personal event in one's life, or a visual image remembered from the past. During World War II Norman Rockwell executed four popular paintings called the *Four Freedoms*. These paintings were reproduced by Lenox China in a collector's-plate series, and the quiltmaker recalled these moving scenes as she began to create her design. Freedom of Speech, Freedom of Worship, Freedom from Want, and Freedom from Fear were important themes to be included in patriotic quilts. This first quilt centers on the Statue of Liberty standing on Liberty Island. The shape of old Fort Wood is outlined in gold. A striking inner border of white stars on a dark-blue background adds visual interest. Each star has been embroidered with the name of a state and the date that it was admitted to the Union. Julia French had little difficulty assembling the quilt top. The actual quilting, however, did not go as easily. She began quilting on November 23, 1985, the birthday of one of her daughters and completed it on January 10, 1986, the birthday of a second daughter. She found the experience so rewarding that she plans to make a quilt for each of her seven children. She has other plans for the future: "In ten years I'm going to repeat the quilt. I may make a few changes in the pattern. I just want to see what I can do with experience."

My New Country, My New Flag, My New Freedom by Beth J. Ide, Belmont, New Hampshire. 1985. 71″ x 71″.
Cottons and polyester blends. The artist chose to "use synthetic fabrics for the sky because I wanted the
special quality of airiness that could be achieved with them and for the flag because most flags today are
actually made from polyester." When designing this quilt, Beth Ide decided to use the Statue of Liberty as the
central design motif, for it is the single most familiar image known to the immigrant. "It provides comfort to
those who have no real idea of what the future will bring." She chose to place the statue and the figure of the
female immigrant within an oval, for she felt this would provide a central vertical focus for the design. The
outside border of the quilt is surrounded by 100 lighted candles, one for each year since the installation of the
Statue of Liberty. At each corner is a red star—a symbol of hope—and four stylized pineapples symbolizing
hospitality. When the quilt was started in April 1985, the artist's husband was most enthusiastic about her efforts.
"At one point I became very discouraged and decided not to go on. He insisted that I keep going. My husband
passed away suddenly while on a trip before the quilt was completed. I finished the quilt in his honor. He would
be so pleased to know that this piece was chosen by a national panel of judges to represent the state of New
Hampshire in The Great American Quilt Contest."

America the Beautiful by Judy B. Dales, Boonton Township, New Jersey. 1985–1986. 71½" x 71½". Cotton and cotton blends. The handsome design for this beautiful quilt was inspired by the song "America the Beautiful," and it depicts the artist's "interpretation of the 'amber waves' of grain, fruited plain, spacious skies, purple mountain majesties, and shining seas along with the 'Lady of Liberty.'" When an artist happily achieves a comfortable design, the work often goes quickly. "The quilt went together faster and more satisfactorily than any other I've done. I had originally planned to use an interesting print for the borders, but after several frustrating shopping excursions decided to piece it instead. Naturally this added an extra week's worth of work. I started working on this quilt November 6, 1985, and finished it January 9, 1986. I worked an average of ten hours a day, excluding one week at Christmas. I prefer piecework to appliqué; consequently, my entire design is pieced. I only had to resort to appliqué for one area of detail on the base of the Statue. I was not sure if it was possible to piece such an intricate design, so I am especially pleased at how successfully it turned out." Judy Dales has been quilting for fifteen years. She is a member of the Garden State Quilters, Vice President of the New Jersey Quilting Teachers, a member of the National Quilting Association, American Quilters Society, Tri-State Quilt Teachers, New Jersey Design Craftsmen, and the American Craft Council. She was granted the 1984 Craft Fellowship Award from the New Jersey Council on the Arts.

Liberty—Promise of America by Carol Meyer, Albuquerque, New Mexico. 1985–1986. 69″ x 69″. Cotton and printed cottons. Many quiltmakers are also recognized artists in other fields. Stained glass was the inspiration for this unusual textile. The composition is centered by the Statue of Liberty. She stands on a pedestal that is embellished with appliqué figures representing people of all races lifting their arms toward the promise of America—liberty and freedom for all. The inner borders emphasize the vertical thrust of the composition. Although Carol Meyer took a few quilt lessons, she considers herself to be essentially self-taught. She has been quilting since 1979, when she finished her first piece. This is her first patriotic quilt. She is a member of several national and local quilting guilds and associations and has won prizes for her needlework at the San Diego Quilt Fair and the New Mexico State Fair.

Reflections on Grandma's Wall by Paula Nadelstern, The Bronx, New York. 1985–1986. 71″ x 71″. Cotton and numerous other fabrics selected for their special decorative quality for use on the frames. The maker revealed her special pleasure: "I love to play with trimmings. It was great fun to make individual frames for each picture in my quilt. I spent many hours on several different trips to the trimming stores on Sixth Avenue in New York City to get what I needed to make the whole thing just right. When I decided to make this quilt I wanted to do something different from everyone else. I knew many would use the Statue of Liberty image at the time of the Liberty Centennial so I focused on the immigrants who came to this country. My mother and my husband's parents came to America as immigrants and passed the Statue of Liberty. Once here and fully established, people recall the Old World and what is important to them in the New World by doing walls of pictures in their home. Walls of pictures are global. My mother has such a wall where all of the grandchildren are included." Paula Nadelstern worked nearly 1,000 hours between October 1, 1985, and January 12, 1986, to complete this quilt.

Sweet Land of Liberty by Jeanne Champion Nowakowski, Hendersonville, North Carolina. 1985. 72″ x 72″. Cotton. Many quiltmakers are inspired by personal experiences or events in their lives. The artist's mother came to America as an immigrant at the age of six. Because of a nighttime arrival, she failed to see the Statue of Liberty. After her family had settled in the Midwest, she always talked about a trip to visit "the great lady." While the artist was in high school, her family journeyed to New York and her mother's dream was fulfilled. The quiltmaker focused on the image of Liberty, for she feels there are many new immigrants to the United States that, like her mother, failed to see the statue upon their arrival in this land of freedom. "Everyone who lives in America feels her influence. Her shadow reaches across the land and her influence spreads everywhere." When designing the quilt the artist used an overhead projector to obtain the central figure. "I had to get it just right. It was so important to me that Liberty be correct." This quilt is only the fourth made by Jeanne Champion Nowakowski. It is her first full-size effort and took approximately six months to stitch. The artist teaches needlework and is a member of several local and national needlework and quilt organizations. She is a biology teacher as well and refers to herself as a pathological teacher.

Focus on Freedom by Lillian A. Twamley, Valley City, North Dakota. 1985–1986. 72″ x 72″. Cotton and cotton blends. The quiltmaker chose to set twelve alternating appliqué and quilted blocks on their points to create the design of her quilt. Appliquéd eagles are worked into the red, white, and blue pieced border. "The scenic blocks depict a cross section of Liberty at different periods of American history. The quilted symbols tie our French/American heritage together. I used the fleur-de-lis to acknowledge the gift of the Statue of Liberty, and the colors red, white, and blue because both the American and the French flags contain these colors." Lillian Twamley made her first quilt in 1976. This Bicentennial effort featured appliquéd figures in period dress from several eras. She is a member of the Valley Quilters. She spent about 1,700 hours researching, drawing, stitching, and finishing this quilt. She has won several awards for her needlework.

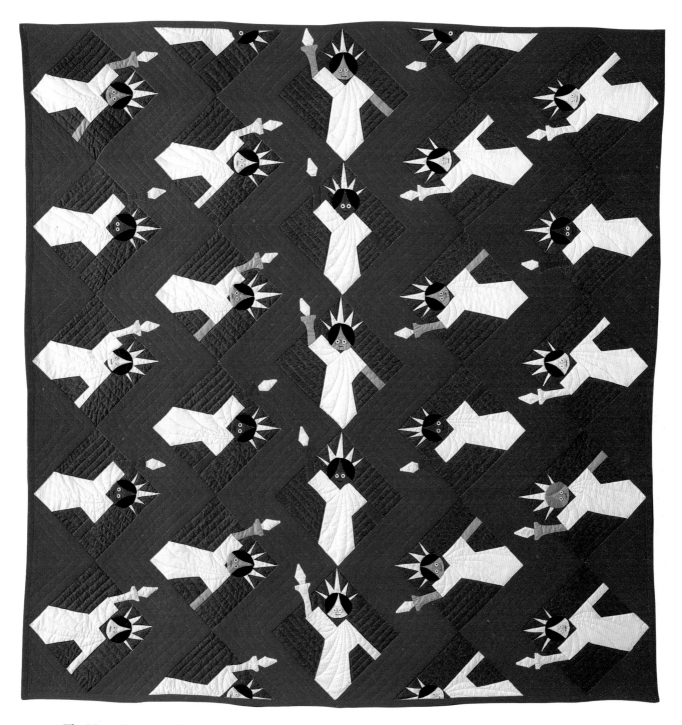

The Many Faces of Liberty by Julia K. Swan, Cambridge, Ohio. 1985–1986. 80″ x 80″. Cotton and polyester blends. Inspiration for the design came from a rag-doll quilt seen many years ago by the artist. The face on each Liberty figure has been created to represent the people of many races that have immigrated to the United States. The artist has personalized her composition by including one Liberty figure with red hair, for nearly all members of her family have red hair, and she wanted them to be represented. While stitching this quilt, the maker discovered that it was nearly twenty inches shorter than the rules for The Great American Quilt Contest specified, so it was taken apart and enlarged. When completed, the quilt was backed with an old bedsheet left from a rooming house operated by the maker's grandmother. Julia Swan has been quilting for nearly six years. This is the only patriotic quilt she has attempted. She has a B.S. degree in Home Economics.

The Essence of Liberty by Mary Kay Boswell, Norman, Oklahoma. 1985. 71¾″ x 71½″. Cotton broadcloth for the appliqué circles and cotton chintz for the remainder of the quilt. The head of the Statue of Liberty and Liberty's torch and book form the central medallion on this quilt. It is surrounded by twelve pictorial circles with symbolic references to traditional American ideas and events, beginning with (from top left moving clockwise) (1) American Indians, (2) Natural Resources, (3) World War II, (4) Agriculture, (5) The Industrial Revolution, (6) The Civil War, (7) Science and Technology, (8) East Meets West, (9) Declaration of Independence, (10) Transportation, (11) Moving West, and (12) World War I. An eagle is quilted into the white upper section of the border and quilted leaves extend down the white sections on the sides. On the white section at the bottom the dates 1886–1986 are quilted. An inner border of white appliqué stars is framed by a gold outer border. Mary Kay Boswell was educated as a home economist and taught for several years. Although she has sewed for over thirty years, this is her first attempt to make a quilt. She borrowed a quilting frame from an aunt, but this proved unsatisfactory. After several tries, she removed the quilt from the frame and ". . . did the whole thing on my lap. This was the only way I could get stitches small enough to be effective."

Give Me Your Huddled Masses by Victoria T. Crawford, Enterprise, Oregon. 1985–1986. 72″ x 72″. Cotton and cotton blends. Liberty is represented in this piece by the quilted crown in the background and by the pieced flame. The artist feels that the Statue "has always symbolized the freedom and the welcoming of the world's people to a better life. In my design, the closer the people are to the crown, the more erect and hopeful the people appear." The quiltmaker decided to create this quilt because she "was interested in exploring new horizons with my hands and therefore mind. The major problem was that of time. I was up to about 3 A.M. every night for one-and-a half months to finish in time. With a new baby, a two-year-old, and a husband, I had to keep my sense of humor." Victoria Crawford spent about 480 hours designing and making this quilt. Her use of pastel-hued fabric seems especially appropriate for her design. She has been quilting for only one year and has never exhibited her quilts or entered a contest before.

The Symbol of Liberty by Donna Barnett-Albert, Lancaster, Pennsylvania. 1985–1986. 72″ x 72″. Cotton and cotton blends. While many of the quilts entered in The Great American Quilt Contest were executed by artists who had never seen the Statue of Liberty, the inspiration for this piece came from a personal experience involving the Lady. "The first mental picture that came to my mind when I read about the contest was ultimately the imagery I used for my quilt. That image came while returning from a trip when I was driving by the Statue of Liberty as the sun was setting behind her. This portrait aroused my emotions. I stared at this American symbol of freedom, and colors, textures, and shapes combined to create a complete visual thought. Designing and creating a quilt is always a changing and growing process. The quilt allows me to 'paint' with cloth. The most significant time came after months of mental ideas and images, sketching, searching and experimenting with colors and fabrics, cutting and fitting, and then, as I began to lay the pieces out, it took life. My initial inspiration materialized." Donna Barnett-Albert graduated from the Philadelphia College of Art in 1969. She has been designing quilts for the past twelve years. Many of her pieces have been illustrated in national magazines and have been seen at invitational quilt exhibitions and shows. She spent about 160 hours designing, piecing, and finishing this quilt.

HOPE

Hope by Barbara Barber, Westerly, Rhode Island. 1985. 72″ x 72″. Cottons. The artist spoke with several immigrant friends before she began to design this quilt. She was interested in what they had seen and what they had felt when they first viewed the Statue of Liberty. A German man who has lived in the United States for many years said that his first impression was that before him was a chance for a new life—hope. The quiltmaker stitched into the borders of the textile the most popular stanza from the well-known poem, *The New Colossus* by Emma Lazarus "...Give me your tired, your poor,/Your huddled masses yearning to breathe free,/The wretched refuse of your teeming shore./Send these, the homeless, tempest-tost to me,/I lift my lamp beside the golden door!" Barbara Barber has been quilting for about ten years. She is a member of the New England Quilters Guild, the Thames River Quilt Guild, the Narragansett Bay Quilt Guild, and was a co-founder of the Nigret Quilt Guild. This quilt represents her second attempt at stitching an entry for The Great American Quilt Contest. This first resulted in a red, white, and blue piece inspired by folk art, which was abandoned before being finished. It took the artist about six weeks to complete this quilt.

Torches of Liberty by Sandra Kuss, Greenville, South Carolina. 1985. 72″ x 72″. Cottons, and block-printed, and commercially printed cottons. Four Liberty torches extend diagonally from the corners of this handsome quilt. The flames converge to form an eight-pointed star. An inner border was created by using the popular nineteenth-century pattern called Ocean Waves, and Delectable Mountains forms the outer border. An olive branch is quilted in the solid areas surrounding the torches. The artist delights in using historic patterns and designs in a contemporary way. She has been quilting for nearly ten years and is a teacher and owner of a shop, where she sells fabrics and quilting supplies. She is a member of the Foothills Piece Makers and the Western North Carolina Quilters Guild.

Liberty Flight by Dawn E. Amos, Rapid City, South Dakota. 1985–1986. 72″ x 72″. Cotton and cotton blends. The artist chose her symbols carefully to acknowledge that we live in a world where natural and man-made materials coexist in a harmonious way. "Liberty is shown enlightening the world. The eagle flies in freedom. Both symbols are man's heritage—be it man-made or God-created." The bright, bold colors signify strength, might, courage, and bravery. Many of the entrants in The Great American Quilt Contest were supported in unusual ways by their families and friends. Dawn Amos said, "Since I waited till the last minute to decide whether or not I could afford the time to make *Liberty Flight* my time was limited. So when the quilt was finally finished, my husband thought we should be reintroduced to each other. I think his major concern was how to get rid of his dishpan hands after a month of doing all the household chores. Now I know I can talk him into a dishwasher —that's electric!" The artist spent 550 hours or thirty-five days of working from between fourteen and sixteen hours a day on this project. She is a professional quiltmaker and quilt designer. She has won several prizes for her work in local and national competitions. She is a member of the Black Hills Quilters Guild.

World Peace Is the Ultimate Liberty by Rosemary Wade, Franklin, Tennessee. 1985. 72″ x 72″. Cotton and cotton prints. The maker of this quilt spent nearly 100 hours in conceptualizing and drawing her design. While some quiltmakers cut paper templates and patterns, she executed her work entirely freehand. In the top right corner there is a quilted outline of a face—a spiritual being symbolizing prayer. In the bottom left corner there are several quilted hands releasing doves, symbolizing peace. Some artists choose to use thread of contrasting colors to emphasize their quilting. Others like Rosemary Wade prefer the subtleties of matching the thread to the fabrics. She has personalized her textile by appliquéing roses instead of stars around the torch. The artist enjoys using solid color, crisp outline quilting, and dramatic prints in all of her compositions. Rosemary Wade pursues the arts in many areas. She paints watercolors, is a home sewer, and enjoys both needlepoint and embroidery. She views quilting as the most satisfying of all of her artistic pursuits. While she worked on this quilt, the artist's sons, aged five and seven, often came to observe her progress. They at first asked if it was "...a picture of King Tut" as the figure had no face. She replied, "No, it's Queen Tut." The name stuck, and the quilt will forever be referred to as "Queen Tut's portrait" in the Wade home. The artist belongs to several local and national quilt organizations and is a professional quilt designer. She maintains a shop, Strickly Amish, which features quilts made by the Amish in Ohio, Pennsylvania, and Kentucky.

Freedom to Dream by Anita Murphy, Kountze, Texas. 1985–1986. 72″ x 72″. Cottons and various blends. The artist enjoys incorporating in her quilts fabrics that have been given to her by friends. The ocean was made from drapery fabric she saved for over eight years. The ships' landing was fashioned from a shampoo cape that was new over a decade ago. Over 580 one- and one-half-inch squares were assembled to make the inner border, and the outside border is a printed paisley. The artist revealed, "...I have a terrible amount of fabric: everywhere there is fabric. You know, there are alcoholics...I guess I am a fabricholic." Pictorial quilts are of most interest to this artist, who is also a well-known teacher and lecturer. She feels, "...a pictorial quilt lets you convey a message. As they say, a picture is worth a thousand words." This quilt was completed in a surprisingly short period of time—just thirty-six days. On many days, Anita Murphy worked over eighteen hours in a single sitting. While her husband was in the hospital in the emergency room, the doctors were persuaded to turn up the lights so she could continue with her quilting. Anita Murphy is a member of several national quilt organizations and is founder of the Beaumont Quilt Guild. Since 1980, when she and her husband sold their family business, she has devoted most of her time to quilting.

Peace Piece: Can Liberty Exist Without a Planet? by Ione Bissonnette, Richford, Vermont. 1985–1986. 72″ x 72″. 100% cotton and satin acetate. The theme of this quilt has a very special meaning to the artist; it is a visual expression of her concern for universal peace. The figure of the woman gestures in a manner similar to the Statue of Liberty. She holds the world in her hand and bows in supplication. Her mission is to call attention to the endangered state of the planet Earth. She trembles before the threat of nuclear war and ecological extinction. The birds and fish represent the innocent creatures of the earth and are shown moving excitedly and fearfully. They cry out a warning to those responsible for the future. In this quilt flowers are a symbol of hope. Love is represented by the two hearts behind the central design, for love alone is a way out of our current dilemma. Ione Bissonnette, a self-taught quiltmaker, never sells her work, but prefers to give it to family and special friends. This quilt is her first patriotic effort, and it is also her first attempt at pictorial appliqué. She recalls her efforts to create this piece as "...a very intense and emotional event in my life."

The Celebration by Violet S. Larsen, Portsmouth, Virginia. 1985–1986. 72″ x 72″. Cotton and cotton blends. This quite extraordinary piece is beautifully conceived. The artist wrote of her composition: "It is nighttime and the viewer joins the Lady to watch the fireworks in celebration of her 100th birthday. The old quilt pattern Storm at Sea is drafted in perspective to give a feeling of distance and to give movement to the waves. Five ducks, one for each of the five boroughs, are pieced into the water. Nearly 700 plastic templates had to be made to finish this quilt." The artist and her husband are native New Yorkers and love the Lady. Their parents immigrated to this country from Norway and landed at Ellis Island. The artist has been quilting for eleven years and spent nearly eight months on this piece. She is a member of the Tidewater Quilters Guild and the American Quilters Society. One of her favorite pastimes is making jointed teddy bears.

Liberty in America by Ruth Carol Coombe, Edmonds, Washington. 1985–1986. 72″ x 72″. Cotton and cotton blends. Four basic designs associated with the Statue of Liberty provide the central focus for this quilt: the head of the Lady; her lighted torch—a beacon for the downtrodden; her book inscribed *JULY IV MDCCLXXVI*; and the outline of Bedloe's Island, on which the Statue stands in New York Harbor. This bold concept is made even stronger by the striking colors used to create this fabric painting. Note especially the pieced-work map of the USA that shows through the openings of Liberty's tiara. Ruth Coombe has been quilting for nearly ten years. She spent approximately 500 hours designing and making this quilt. Other pieces by her have won prizes and awards. She is a member of Quilters Anonymous.

Facsimile of American Symbols by Hazel B. Reed Ferrell, Middlebourne, West Virginia. 1985. 72″ x 72″. Cotton and mixed cotton with polyester. When the artist began to conceptualize the design for this quilt, she found it an easy task. "I chose American symbols because I'm just a full-blooded American. I did the central square with the Liberty figure first. My family was so thrilled! They just knew I was going to place in the Great American Quilt Contest. I next decided to include the Confederate flag and the American flag along with two presidential wreaths, one surrounding a silhouette of George Washington and the other a silhouette of Ronald Reagan. The eagle and the American shield and the eagle and the Liberty Bell balance my composition. The doves at the four corners symbolize peace. I have included a dedication on the lower outside edge of the quilt: *To your image Miss Liberty. In memory of all servicemen who bid you farewell and never return to say hello.* Hazel Reed is a self-taught quilter, although she grew up in a family where nearly all of the women made bedcovers. She remembers as a young child helping her grandmother and her mother make quilts. "I'm sure they took out my stitches at first. It takes a lot to learn to do good quilting. I like doing patriotic quilts. I have one in the Gerald R. Ford Presidential Museum in Grand Rapids, Michigan, that I did at the time of the Bicentennial." The artist is a member of The National Quilting Association and the American Quilting Association.

Bright Hopes, Bright Promise by Carol Butzke, Slinger, Wisconsin. 1986. 72″ x 72″. Cotton and printed cotton. The artist found her inspiration for the design of this quilt in "the immigrants themselves and what they must have had to go through to start a new life here. Also, my interest in the old traditional patterns and the generations of women who carried on the art of quilting" was a major reason for her work on the piece. Shortly after the quilt was finished, the maker's five-year-old son sauntered into the family room one evening and wanted to know if the new "snuggle blanket" was ready to sleep under. She promptly covered him with her work of art. "After all, that's what quilts are for." This quilt might well be the only piece from The Great American Quilt Contest that has actually been used. Carol Butzke has been quilting for six years and enjoys being a member of Wisconsin Quilters, Inc. and Stitch Quilt Guild. Because her young children take so much of her time, she never recorded the hours spent on this piece. She has won Best in Show, Viewers' Choice, and several blue ribbons at local and state quilt shows.

The Lady by Donna Schneider, Rawlins, Wyoming. 1985–1986. 71¾″ x 72″. Unbleached muslin. This quilt is one of the few "white-work" pieces entered in The Great American Quilt Contest. White work of various types was particularly popular in the early nineteenth century, for it was a means by which accomplished needlewomen could display their special skills. The artist has used the Statue of Liberty as the central motif in her composition. The words *Centennial, Justice, Liberty,* and *Freedom* are quilted in the wide borders. The dates *1886* and *1986* are stitched at top left and right, while *USA* and *July 4, 1776* are quilted at bottom left and right. Liberty's torch, crown, and the shackles of tyranny at the Statue's feet have been stuffed. The artist is very proud of this quilt "because I tried and overcame so many problems every step of the process and still ended with a beautiful quilt. I removed many stitches because they were too big or long and just kept at it, till I was finally pleased. Removing the marking pen completely was a special problem. I even shed tears when I had to machine wash the finished quilt. But look at it now, prettier and brighter." Donna Schneider has been quilting seriously for about four years. She worked two full months—day and night on this quilt. She is a member of the Methodist Women's Velvet Bells.

101

Humble Beginnings by Cathy Patton, Haddonfield, New Jersey. (Members of the military services were able to compete in The Great American Quilt Contest through the special category, United States Possessions, Territories, and Military Bases Abroad. The artist is currently located in Vogelweh, Germany.) 1985–1986. 72″ x 72″. Cotton and cotton blends. The central section of this quilt is made of a single piece of cloth. The borders were added and then quilted. "This counterpane-type quilt of cream tiger cloth and brown broadcloth has been stitched in brown thread." The elaborate quilting includes a central figure of the Statue of Liberty and a ship in full sail. It was on such vessels that many of the immigrants to America arrived. Several quilted figures in the lower section of the quilt refer to the immigrant experience. Included is a figure of a black slave girl, a Puritan woman, and a nineteenth-century man.